D1488114

To

_____

From

_____

Promises
Made...
Promises
Kept...

I pledge my love

100 Devotions for
A Husband and Wife

The quoted ideas expressed in this book (but not scripture verses) are not, in all cases, exact quotations, as some have been edited for clarity and brevity. In all cases, the author has attempted to maintain the speaker's original intent. In some cases, quoted material for this book was obtained from secondary sources, primarily print media. While every effort was made to ensure the accuracy of these sources, the accuracy cannot be guaranteed. For additions, deletions, corrections or clarifications in future editions of this text, please write FAMILY CHRISTIAN STORES.

Scripture quotations are taken from:

The Holy Bible, King James Version

The Holy Bible, New International Version (NIV) Copyright © 1973, 1978, 1984, by International Bible Society. Used by permission of Zondervan Publishing House. All rights reserved.

The Holy Bible, New King James Version (NKJV) Copyright © 1982 by Thomas Nelson, Inc. Used by permission.

The New American Standard Bible®, (NASB) Copyright © 1960, 1962, 1963, 1968, 1971, 1972, 1973, 1975, 1977, 1995 by The Lockman Foundation. Used by permission.

Holy Bible, New Living Translation, (NLT)copyright © 1996. Used by permission of Tyndale House Publishers, Inc., Wheaton, Illinois 60189. All rights reserved.

The Message (MSG)- This edition issued by contractual arrangement with NavPress, a division of The Navigators, U.S.A. Originally published by NavPress in English as THE MESSAGE: The Bible in Contemporary Language copyright 2002-2003 by Eugene Peterson. All rights reserved.

New Century Version®. (NCV) Copyright © 1987, 1988, 1991 by Word Publishing, a division of Thomas Nelson, Inc. All rights reserved. Used by permission.

The Holman Christian Standard Bible™ (HCSB) Copyright © 1999, 2000, 2001 by Holman Bible Publishers. Used by permission.

Cover Design by Kim Russell / Wahoo Designs
Page Layout by Bart Dawson

ISBN 978-1-60587-180-6

Promises
Made...
Promises
Kept...

100 Devotions for
A Husband and Wife

PROMISES MADE...PROMISES KEPT...100 DAILY DEVOTIONS

PROMISES KEPT...100 DAILY DEVOTIONS

PROMISES MADE...PROMISES KEPT...100 DAILY DEVOTIONS

PROMISES MADE...PROMISES KEPT...

Introduction

Now these three remain: faith, hope, and love.
But the greatest of these is love.
1 Corinthians 13:13 Holman CSB

"But the greatest of these is love"—seven familiar words that remind us of a simple truth: God places a high priority on love . . . and so should we. Faith is important, of course. So, too, is hope. But love is more important still.

This text is a celebration of Christian love and Christian marriage. It contains 100 chapters, each of which serves as a reminder that God intends that His Word be used as a blueprint for every marriage, including yours.

When you make God's Word the centerpiece of your family and your life, you'll feel differently about your spouse, you'll feel differently about your children, you'll feel differently about your world, and you'll feel differently about your future.

So make this promise to yourself, to your spouse, and to your God: promise that you will use the ideas on these pages to make your marriage a model of Christian love. Promise, also, that you will seek God's guidance for your marriage, and that you will trust the guidance that He gives. When you do, your Heavenly Father will bless you and your family today, tomorrow, and forever.

With All My Heart

Love one another fervently with a pure heart.

1 Peter 1:22 NKJV

Are you genuinely excited about your marriage? Are you committed to your spouse with all your heart? Do you feel good about yourself, your spouse, your kids, and your home life? And do you see each day as a glorious opportunity for your family to serve God and to do His will? Hopefully so. After all, you and your family members were created in God's image, and He has blessed you in more ways than you can count. Now, it's your job to thank Him with words and with deeds.

Psalm 100 reminds us that, as believers, we have every reason to celebrate: "Shout for joy to the LORD, all the earth. Worship the LORD with gladness" (v. 1-2 NIV). And as you consider the treasures that God has given you—starting with (but not limited to) your marriage and your family—give thanks to your Creator. And when you're finished thanking your Father in heaven, give thanks to your spouse!

MORE THOUGHTS FOR TODAY

The Christian way of life lends stability to marriage because its principles and values naturally produce harmony.

James Dobson

The marital love is a thing pure as light, sacred as a temple, lasting as the world.

Jeremy Taylor

We've grown to be one soul—two parts; our lives are so intertwined that when some passion stirs your heart, I feel the quake in mine.

Gloria Gaither

And may the Lord make you increase and abound in love to one another and to all.

1 Thessalonians 3:12 NKJV

OUR PRAYER FOR TODAY

Dear Lord, Your Word teaches us that our marriage
is both sacred and eternal. We thank You, Father,
for the love that we share today, tomorrow, and forever.
Amen

DAY 2

Promises Made,
Promises Kept

Those who trust in the LORD are as secure as Mount Zion;
they will not be defeated but will endure forever.

Psalm 125:1 NLT

"Promises made, promises kept." Husbands and wives should place these four words on their hearts because the best marriages are built upon a foundation of honesty and trust. Without trust, marriages soon begin to wither; with trust, marriages soon begin to flourish.

For Christians, honesty is the right policy because it's God's policy. God's Word makes it clear: "Lying lips are an abomination to the Lord, but those who deal truthfully are His delight" (Proverbs 12:22 NKJV).

Sometimes, honesty is difficult; sometimes, honesty is painful; sometimes, honesty makes us feel uncomfortable. Despite these temporary feelings of discomfort, we must make honesty the hallmark of all our relationships; otherwise, we invite needless suffering into our own lives and into the lives of those we love.

Do you want your love to last forever? Then you and your spouse must commit to build a relationship based upon mutual trust and unerring truth. Both of you deserve nothing less . . . and neither, for that matter, does God.

MORE THOUGHTS FOR TODAY

Trust is like "money in the bank" in a marriage. There must be a reasonable amount of it on deposit to ensure the security of a marital union.

Ed Young

When men cease to be faithful to their God, he who expects to find them faithful to each other will be much disappointed.

George Horne

Many words do not satisfy the soul; but a good life eases the mind and a clean conscience inspires great trust in God.

Thomas à Kempis

The Good News shows how God makes people right with himself—that it begins and ends with faith. As the Scripture says, "But those who are right with God will live by trusting in him."

Romans 1:17 NCV

OUR PRAYER FOR TODAY

Dear Lord, as we build our marriage day by day,
we will build it upon trust—
trust in each other and trust in You.
Amen

The Christ-centered Marriage

You shall have no other gods before Me.

Exodus 20:3 NKJV

The Bible makes it clear that in marriage, as in every other aspect of life, God should come first. The words of Matthew 6:33 remind us that we should "seek first the kingdom of God and His righteousness." And how can we honor God in this way? By allowing His Son to reign over our hearts and our marriages.

A Christ-centered marriage is an exercise in faith, love, fidelity, trust, understanding, forgiveness, caring, sharing, and encouragement. It requires empathy, tenderness, patience, and perseverance. It is the union of two Christian adults, both of whom are willing to compromise and, when appropriate, to apologize. A Christ-centered marriage requires large quantities of common sense, common courtesy, and uncommon caring. Such a marriage is a joy to behold, a joy to experience, and a blessing forever.

Does Christ truly preside over your marriage, or does He occupy a position of lesser importance? The answer to that question will determine the quality and direction of your lives. When both you and your spouse allow Jesus to reign over your lives, Christ will bless you and your family in wonderful, unexpected ways. So today and every day, make your marriage a model of Christian love, respect, and service.

MORE THOUGHTS FOR TODAY

As I grew older, I realized that my parents' love for one another was deeper than just the look in their eyes each time one of them came into the room. Their love was based on more than their physical and emotional attraction. It was based on solid, uncompromising commitment, first to Jesus Christ, and second to the institution of marriage.

Gigi Graham Tchividjian

A man's communication with his wife is dependent upon his communication with the Father.

Stormie Omartian

A successful marriage is always triangle: a man, a woman, and God.

Cecil Myers

So they are no longer two, but one flesh. Therefore what God has joined together, man must not separate.

Matthew 19:6 Holman CSB

OUR PRAYER FOR TODAY

Dear Lord, today, we invite You to reign over
our marriage. May Your will be our will. May Your Word
be our guide, and may we grow in faith
and in wisdom this day and every day.
Amen

A Cause for Celebration

Be happy with the wife you married when you were young.
She gives you joy, as your fountain gives you water.

Proverbs 5:18 NCV

A Christian marriage should be cause for celebration, but sometimes we don't feel much like celebrating. In fact, when the weight of the world seems to bear down upon our shoulders, celebration may be the last thing on our minds . . . but it shouldn't be. As God's children, we are all blessed beyond measure on good days and bad. This day is a non-renewable resource—once it's gone, it's gone forever. We should give thanks for this day while using it for the glory of God.

What will be your attitude today? Will you be fearful, angry, bored, or worried? Will you infect your marriage with the twin blights of cynicism and bitterness? Are you a person who celebrates your life and your marriage? Hopefully so! After all, God has richly blessed you, and He wants you to rejoice in His gifts. But, God will not force His joy upon you; you must claim it for yourself.

So today, and every day hereafter, celebrate the life that God has given you. Think optimistically about yourself, your marriage, your family, and your future. Give thanks to the One who has given you everything, and trust in your heart that He wants to give you so much more.

MORE THOUGHTS FOR TODAY

Attitude is all-important. Let the soul take a quiet attitude of faith and love toward God, and from there on, the responsibility is God's. He will make good on His commitments.

A. W. Tozer

The hard part about being a praying wife is maintaining a pure heart. If you have resentment, anger, unforgiveness, or an ungodly attitude—even if there's good reason for it—you'll have a difficult time seeing answers to your prayers. But if you can release those feelings to God in total honesty, there is nothing that can change a marriage more dramatically.

Stormie Omartian

He who finds a wife finds what is good and receives favor from the Lord.

Proverbs 18:22 NIV

OUR PRAYER FOR TODAY

We thank You, Lord, for the gift of marriage.
And we thank You for the love, the care, the devotion,
and the genuine friendship that we share
this day and forever.
Amen

Practical Christianity

Therefore, get your minds ready for action,
being self-disciplined, and set your hope completely
on the grace to be brought to you
at the revelation of Jesus Christ.

1 Peter 1:13 Holman CSB

As Christians, we must do our best to ensure that our actions are accurate reflections of our beliefs. Our theology must be demonstrated, not only by our words but, more importantly, by our actions. In short, we should be practical believers, quick to act whenever we see an opportunity to serve God.

Are you the kind of practical Christian who is willing to dig in and do what needs to be done when it needs to be done? If so, congratulations: God acknowledges your service and blesses it. But if you find yourself more interested in the fine points of theology than in the needs of your neighbors, it's time to rearrange your priorities. God needs believers who are willing to roll up their sleeves and go to work for Him. Count yourself among that number. Theology is a good thing unless it interferes with God's work. And it's up to you to make certain that your theology doesn't.

MORE THOUGHTS FOR TODAY

Do noble things, do not dream them all day long.

Charles Kingsley

A bird does not know it can fly before it uses its wings. We learn God's love in our hearts as soon as we act upon it.

Corrie ten Boom

Action springs not from thought, but from a readiness for responsibility.

Dietrich Bonhoeffer

Do what God's teaching says; when you only listen and do nothing, you are fooling yourselves.

James 1:22 NCV

OUR PRAYER FOR TODAY

Dear Lord, we have heard Your Word, and we have felt Your presence in our hearts; let us act accordingly. Let our words and deeds serve as a testimony to the changes You have made in our lives. Let us praise You, Father, by following in the footsteps of Your Son, and let others see Him through us.

Amen

Parents Shape Eternity

*Parents, don't come down too hard on your children
or you'll crush their spirits.*

Colossians 3:21 MSG

If you're a parent in our 21st-century world, you need keen insight, prudent foresight, and sharp eyesight. But that's not all. You also need discipline, patience, prayer, and a willingness to teach.

Parents are their kids' most important instructors. Daniel Webster wrote, "If we work in marble, it will perish; if we work upon brass, time will efface it; if we rear temples, they will crumble into dust; but if we work upon immortal minds and instill in them just principles, we are then engraving upon tablets which no time will efface, but which will brighten and brighten to all eternity." These words remind us of the glorious opportunities that are available to those of us who teach our children well.

Are you and your spouse teaching from the same curriculum? And does that curriculum begin and end with The Book. Hopefully so, because that's exactly what your children need.

Do you sincerely seek to leave a lasting legacy for generations to come? If so, you must start by teaching your children the ways and the Word of God. And remember always that your most enduring lessons are not the ones you teach with words; they are the ones you teach by example. When you obey God's commandments and trust His promises, your life will be a shining lesson for your children . . . and for theirs.

MORE THOUGHTS FOR TODAY

The Creator has given to us the awesome responsibility of representing Him to our children. Our Heavenly Father is a God of unlimited love, and our children must become acquainted with His mercy and tenderness through our own love toward them.

James Dobson

Train up a child in the way he should go: and when he is old, he will not depart from it.

Proverbs 22:6 KJV

OUR PRAYER FOR TODAY

Dear Lord, help us be responsible, loving, godly parents. Let us teach our children to worship You and to study Your Word. When we are uncertain, Lord, give us wisdom. And, in everything that we do and say, let us be worthy examples to our family members every day that we live. Amen

He Leads

However, I did give them this command:
Obey Me, and then I will be your God,
and you will be My people. You must walk in every
way I command you so that it may go well with you.

Jeremiah 7:23 Holman CSB

When we genuinely open our hearts to God, He speaks to us through a small, still voice within. When He does, we can listen, or not. When we pay careful attention to the Father, He leads us along a path of His choosing; a path that leads to abundance, peace, joy, and eternal life. But when we choose to ignore God, we select a path that is not His, and we must endure the consequences of our shortsightedness.

Today, focus your thoughts and your prayers on the path that God intends for you to take. When you do, your loving Heavenly Father will speak to your heart. When He does, listen carefully . . . and trust Him.

When we truly walk with God throughout our day, life slowly starts to fall into place.

Bill Hybels

MORE THOUGHTS FOR TODAY

Only by walking with God can we hope to find the path that leads to life.

John Eldredge

It is God to whom and with whom we travel, while He is the End of our journey, He is also at every stopping place.

Elisabeth Elliot

Trust in the LORD with all your heart; do not depend on your own understanding. Seek his will in all you do, and he will direct your paths.

Proverbs 3:5-6 NLT

OUR PRAYER FOR TODAY

Dear Lord, help us find the path that You intend
for us to follow. We can live courageously, Father,
because we know that You are leading us to a place
of Your choosing . . . and where You lead,
we will follow.
Amen

Whom to Please?

Do you think I am trying to make people accept me?
No, God is the One I am trying to please.
Am I trying to please people? If I still wanted to please people,
I would not be a servant of Christ.

Galatians 1:10 NCV

Rick Warren observed, "Those who follow the crowd usually get lost in it." We know these words to be true, but oftentimes we fail to live by them. Instead of trusting God for guidance, we imitate our neighbors and suffer the consequences. Instead of seeking to please our Father in heaven, we strive to please our peers, with decidedly mixed results.

Whom will you try to please today: your God or your friends? Your obligation is most certainly not to neighbors, to friends, or even to family members. Your obligation is to an all-knowing, all-powerful God. You must seek to please Him first and always. No exceptions.

Applause is the spur of noble minds, the end and aim of weak ones.

Charles Caleb Colton

MORE THOUGHTS FOR TODAY

You must never sacrifice your relationship with God for the sake of a relationship with another person.

Charles Stanley

Many people never receive God's best for them because they are addicted to the approval of others.

Joyce Meyer

My dear friends, don't let public opinion influence how you live out our glorious, Christ-originated faith.

James 2:1 MSG

OUR PRAYER FOR TODAY

Dear Lord, today we will worry less about pleasing
other people and more about pleasing You. We will honor
You with our thoughts, our actions, and our prayers.
And we will worship You, Father, with thanksgiving
in our hearts, this day and forever.
Amen

Perspective for Today

Make me to hear joy and gladness....

Psalm 51:8 KJV

If a temporary loss of perspective has left you worried, exhausted, or both, it's time to readjust your thought patterns. Negative thoughts are habit-forming; thankfully, so are positive ones. With practice, you can form the habit of focusing on God's priorities and your own possibilities. When you do, you'll soon discover that you will spend less time fretting about your challenges and more time praising God for His gifts.

When you call upon the Lord and prayerfully seek His will, He will give you wisdom and perspective. When you make God's priorities your priorities, He will direct your steps and calm your fears. So today and every day hereafter, pray for a sense of balance and perspective. And remember: no problems are too big for God—and that includes yours.

The proper perspective creates within us a spirit of reaching outside of ourselves with joy and enthusiasm.

Luci Swindoll

MORE THOUGHTS FOR TODAY

Instead of being frustrated and overwhelmed by all that is going on in our world, go to the Lord and ask Him to give you His eternal perspective.

Kay Arthur

Earthly fears are no fears at all. Answer the big questions of eternity, and the little questions of life fall into perspective.

Max Lucado

My cup runs over. Surely goodness and mercy shall follow me all the days of my life; and I will dwell in the house of the Lord Forever.

Psalm 23:5-6 NKJV

OUR PRAYER FOR TODAY

Dear Lord, sometimes, the world's perspective can lead us astray. Give us guidance, wisdom, and perspective. And keep us mindful, Father, that Your reality is the ultimate reality, and that Your truth is the ultimate truth, now and forever.

Amen

When the Answer Is No

Rejoice evermore. Pray without ceasing.
In every thing give thanks: for this is the will of God
in Christ Jesus concerning you.

1 Thessalonians 5:16-18 KJV

God answers our prayers. What God does not do is this: He does not always answer our prayers as soon as we might like, and He does not always answer our prayers by saying "Yes." God isn't an order-taker, and He's not some sort of cosmic vending machine. Sometimes—even when we want something very badly—our loving Heavenly Father responds to our requests by saying "No", and we must accept His answer, even if we don't understand it.

God answers prayers not only according to our wishes but also according to His master plan. We cannot know that plan, but we can know the Planner . . . and we must trust His wisdom, His righteousness, and His love. Always.

If God chooses to remain silent, faith is content.

Ruth Bell Graham

MORE THOUGHTS FOR TODAY

All prayers are answered. We need to distinguish between a
prayer unanswered and one not answered how or when we
would like it to be.

Lloyd Ogilvie

Sometimes what you get turns out to be better than what
you wanted in the first place.

Eve Bunting

The effective prayer of a righteous man can accomplish much.
James 5:16 NASB

OUR PRAYER FOR TODAY

We pray to You, Father, because You desire it and because
we need it. Prayer not only changes things, it changes us.
Help us, Lord, never to face the demands of the day
without first spending time with You.
Amen

Purposeful Living

Whatever you do, do all to the glory of God.

1 Corinthians 10:31 NKJV

E ach morning, as the sun rises in the east, you welcome a new day, one that is filled to the brim with opportunities, with possibilities, and with God. As you contemplate God's blessings in your own life, you should prayerfully seek His guidance for the day ahead.

Discovering God's unfolding purpose for your life is a daily journey, a journey guided by the teachings of God's Holy Word. As you reflect upon God's promises and upon the meaning that those promises hold for you, ask God to lead you throughout the coming day. Let your Heavenly Father direct your steps; concentrate on what God wants you to do now, and leave the distant future in hands that are far more capable than your own: His hands.

The place where God calls you is the place where your deep gladness and the world's deep hunger meet.

Frederick Buechner

MORE THOUGHTS FOR TODAY

The Christian life is not simply following principles but being empowered to fulfill our purpose: knowing and exalting Christ.

Franklin Graham

How much of our lives are, well, so daily. How often our hours are filled with the mundane, seemingly unimportant things that have to be done, whether at home or work. These very "daily" tasks could become a celebration of praise. "It is through consecration," someone has said, "that drudgery is made divine."

Gigi Graham Tchividjian

You're sons of Light, daughters of Day. We live under wide open skies and know where we stand. So let's not sleepwalk through life . . .

1 Thessalonians 5:5-6 MSG

OUR PRAYER FOR TODAY

Dear Lord, You are the Creator of the universe, and we know that Your plan for our lives is grander than we can imagine. Let Your purposes be our purposes, and let us trust in the assurance of Your promises.

Amen

Questions?

We are pressured in every way but not crushed;
we are perplexed but not in despair.

2 Corinthians 4:8 Holman CSB

When you have a question that you simply can't answer, whom do you ask? When you face a difficult decision, to whom do you turn for counsel? To friends? To mentors? To family members? Or do you turn first to the ultimate source of wisdom? The answers to life's Big Questions start with God and with the teachings of His Holy Word.

God's wisdom stands forever. God's Word is a light for every generation. Make it your light as well. Use the Bible as a compass for the next stage of your life's journey. Use it as the yardstick by which your behavior is measured. And as you carefully consult the pages of God's Word, prayerfully ask Him to reveal the wisdom that you need. When you take your concerns to God, He will not turn you away; He will, instead, offer answers that are tested and true. Your job is to ask, to listen, and to trust.

MORE THOUGHTS FOR TODAY

Be to the world a sign that while we as Christians do not have all the answers, we do know and care about the questions.

Billy Graham

We are finding we don't have such a gnawing need to know the answers when we know the Answer.

Gloria Gaither

Questions never threaten the living God, who is constantly calling us, and who affirms for us that love is stronger than hate, blessing stronger than cursing.

Madeleine L'Engle

Stop quarreling with God! If you agree with him, you will have peace at last, and things will go well for you.

Job 22:21 NLT

OUR PRAYER FOR TODAY

Dear God, sometimes this world can be a puzzling place. When we are unsure of our next steps, keep us aware that You are always near. Give us faith, Father, and let us remember that with Your love and Your power, we can live courageously and faithfully today and every day.

Amen

Optimistic Christianity

But if we look forward to something we don't have yet,
we must wait patiently and confidently.

Romans 8:25 NLT

Pessimism and Christianity don't mix. Why? Because Christians have every reason to be optimistic about life here on earth and life eternal. As C. H. Spurgeon observed, "Our hope in Christ for the future is the mainstream of our joy." But sometimes, we fall prey to worry, frustration, anxiety, or sheer exhaustion, and our hearts become heavy. What's needed is plenty of rest, a large dose of perspective, and God's healing touch, but not necessarily in that order.

Today, make this promise to yourself and keep it: vow to be a hope-filled Christian. Think optimistically about your life, your profession, your future, and your students. Trust your hopes, not your fears. Take time to celebrate God's glorious creation. And then, when you've filled your heart with hope and gladness, share your optimism with others. They'll be better for it, and so will you. But not necessarily in that order.

MORE THOUGHTS FOR TODAY

No Christian can be a pessimist, for Christianity is a system of radical optimism.

William Ralph Inge

The Christian lifestyle is not one of legalistic do's and don'ts, but one that is positive, attractive, and joyful.

Vonette Bright

When you affirm big, believe big, and pray big, big things happen.

Norman Vincent Peale

Make me hear joy and gladness.

Psalm 51:8 NKJV

OUR PRAYER FOR TODAY

Thank You, Lord, for Your infinite love.
Make us optimistic Christians, Father, as we place
our hopes and our trust in You. Amen

Renewal

The One who was sitting on the throne said,
"Look! I am making everything new!" Then he said,
"Write this, because these words are true and can be trusted."
Revelation 21:5 NCV

When we genuinely lift our hearts and prayers to God, He renews our strength. Are you almost too weary to lift your head? Then bow it. Offer your concerns and your fears to your Father in Heaven. He is always at your side, offering His love and His strength.

Are you troubled or anxious? Take your anxieties to God in prayer. Are you weak or worried? Delve deeply into God's Holy Word and sense His presence in the quiet moments of the early morning. Are you spiritually exhausted? Call upon fellow believers to support you, and call upon Christ to renew your spirit and your life. Your Savior will never let you down. To the contrary, He will always lift you up if you ask Him to. So what, dear friend, are you waiting for?

Father, for this day, renew within me the gift of the Holy Spirit.

Andrew Murray

MORE THOUGHTS FOR TODAY

When we reach the end of our strength, wisdom, and personal resources, we enter into the beginning of His glorious provisions.

Patsy Clairmont

God specializes in things fresh and firsthand. His plans for you this year may outshine those of the past. He's prepared to fill your days with reasons to give Him praise.

Joni Eareckson Tada

When doubts filled my mind, your comfort gave me renewed hope and cheer.

Psalm 94:19 NLT

OUR PRAYER FOR TODAY

Heavenly Father, sometimes we are troubled, and
sometimes we grow weary. When we are weak, Lord,
give us strength. When we are discouraged, renew us.
When we are fearful, let us feel Your healing touch.
Let us always trust in Your promises, Lord,
and let us draw strength from those promises and from
Your unending love.
Amen

The Importance of Fellowship

You must get along with each other.
You must learn to be considerate of one another,
cultivating a life in common.

1 Corinthians 1:10 MSG

Fellowship with other believers should be an integral part of your everyday life. Your association with fellow Christians should be uplifting, enlightening, encouraging, and consistent.

Are you an active member of your own fellowship? Are you a builder of bridges inside the four walls of your church and outside it? Do you contribute to God's glory by contributing your time and your talents to a close-knit band of believers? Hopefully so. The fellowship of believers is intended to be a powerful tool for spreading God's Good News and uplifting His children. And God intends for you to be a fully contributing member of that fellowship. Your intentions should be the same.

MORE THOUGHTS FOR TODAY

God shows unbridled delight when He sees people acting in ways that honor Him: when He receives worship, when He sees faith demonstrated in the most trying of circumstances, and when He sees tender love shared among His people.

Bill Hybels

In God's economy you will be hard-pressed to find many examples of successful "Lone Rangers."

Luci Swindoll

The Lord Jesus Christ enables us all to be family.

Dennis Swanberg

Don't become partners with those who reject God. How can you make a partnership out of right and wrong? That's not partnership; that's war. Is light best friends with dark?

2 Corinthians 6:14 MSG

OUR PRAYER FOR TODAY

Heavenly Father, You have given us a community of
supporters called the church. Let our fellowship be
a reflection of the love we feel for each other,
the love we feel for our fellow believers,
and the love we feel for You.
Amen

The Power of Encouragement

So encourage each other and give each other strength,
just as you are doing now.

1 Thessalonians 5:11 NCV

Marriage is a team sport, and all of us need occasional pats on the back from our teammate. In the Book of Proverbs, we read that, "A word aptly spoken is like apples of gold in settings of silver" (25:11 NIV). This verse reminds us that the words we speak can and should be beautiful offerings to those we love.

All of us have the power to enrich the lives of our loved ones. Sometimes, when we feel uplifted and secure, we find it easy to speak words of encouragement and hope. Other times, when we are discouraged or tired, we can scarcely summon the energy to uplift ourselves, much less anyone else. But, as loving Christians, our obligation is clear: we must always measure our words carefully as we use them to benefit others and to glorify our Father in heaven.

God intends that we speak words of kindness, wisdom, and truth, no matter our circumstances, no matter our emotions. When we do, we share a priceless gift with our loved ones, and we give glory to the One who gave His life for us. As believers, we must do no less.

MORE THOUGHTS FOR TODAY

Your mate doesn't live by bread alone; he or she needs to be "buttered" from time to time.

Zig Ziglar

Words. Do you fully understand their power? Can any of us really grasp the mighty force behind the things we say? Do we stop and think before we speak, considering the potency of the words we utter?

Joni Eareckson Tada

What are your spouse's dreams? What are you doing to encourage or discourage those dreams?

Dennis Swanberg

Encourage each other. Live in harmony and peace. Then the God of love and peace will be with you.

2 Corinthians 13:11 NLT

OUR PRAYER FOR TODAY

Dear Heavenly Father, because we are Your children,
we are blessed. You have loved us eternally, cared for us
faithfully, and saved us through the gift of Your Son Jesus.
Just as You have lifted us up, Lord, let us lift up others in
a spirit of encouragement and optimism and hope.
And, if we can help a fellow traveler, even in a small way,
Dear Lord, may the glory be Yours.
Amen

Today's Opportunities

Therefore, as we have opportunity,
we must work for the good of all, especially for those
who belong to the household of faith.

Galatians 6:10 Holman CSB

A re you excited about the opportunities of today and thrilled by the possibilities of tomorrow? Do you confidently expect God to lead you to a place of abundance, peace, and joy? And, when your days on earth are over, do you expect to receive the priceless gift of eternal life? If you trust God's promises, and if you have welcomed God's Son into your heart, then you believe that your future is intensely and eternally bright.

Today, as you prepare to meet the duties of everyday life, pause and consider God's promises. And then think for a moment about the wonderful future that awaits all believers, including you. God has promised that your future is secure. Trust that promise, and celebrate the life of abundance and eternal joy that is now yours through Christ.

MORE THOUGHTS FOR TODAY

Don't waste today's time cluttering up tomorrow's opportunities with yesterday's troubles.

Barbara Johnson

Life is a glorious opportunity.

Billy Graham

Every day we live is a priceless gift of God, loaded with possibilities to learn something new, to gain fresh insights.

Dale Evans Rogers

Let us not lose heart in doing good, for in due time we shall reap if we do not grow weary. So then, while we have opportunity, let us do good to all men, and especially to those who are of the household of the faith.

Galatians 6:9-10 NASB

OUR PRAYER FOR TODAY

Dear Lord, as we travel through this life together,
we will travel with You. Whatever this day may bring,
we will thank You for the opportunity to live abundantly.
We will lean upon You, Father—and trust You—
this day and forever.
Amen

Comforting Others

*Blessed be the God and Father of our Lord Jesus Christ,
the Father of mercies and the God of all comfort. He comforts
us in all our affliction, so that we may be able to comfort those
who are in any kind of affliction, through the comfort
we ourselves receive from God.*

2 Corinthians 1:3-4 Holman CSB

We live in a world that is, on occasion, a frightening place. Sometimes, we sustain life-changing losses that are so profound and so tragic that it seems we could never recover. But, with God's help and with the help of encouraging family members and friends, we can recover.

In times of need, friends comfort friends. Our task, as Christians, is to comfort our families and friends by sharing not only our own courage but also the peace and assurance of our Lord and Savior, Christ Jesus. As the renowned revivalist Vance Havner observed, "No journey is complete that does not lead through some dark valleys. We can properly comfort others only with the comfort wherewith we ourselves have been comforted of God."

In times of adversity, we are wise to remember the words of Jesus, who, when He walked on the waters, reassured His disciples, saying, "Take courage! It is I. Don't be afraid" (Matthew 14:27 NIV). Then, with Christ on His throne and trusted friends at our side, we can face our fears with courage and faith.

MORE THOUGHTS FOR TODAY

Discouraged people don't need critics. They hurt enough already. They don't need more guilt or piled-on distress. They need encouragement. They need a refuge, a willing, caring, available someone.

Charles Swindoll

So often we think that to be encouragers we have to produce great words of wisdom when, in fact, a few simple syllables of sympathy and an arm around the shoulder can often provide much needed comfort.

Florence Littauer

Carry each other's burdens, and in this way you will fulfill the law of Christ.

Galatians 6:2 NIV

OUR PRAYER FOR TODAY

Heavenly Father, sometimes this world can be a difficult place indeed. Let us be beacons of encouragement to those who have lost hope. Let us comfort those who grieve. And let us share Your love and spread Your Word to a world that needs both.

Amen

A Willingness to Listen

My dear brothers and sisters,
always be willing to listen and slow to speak.

James 1:19 NCV

What a blessing it is when our loved ones genuinely seek to understand who we are and what we think. Just as we wish to be understood by others, so, too, should we seek to understand the hopes and dreams of our spouses and our family members.

Are you in the habit of listening to your mate? Do you listen carefully (not superficially), and do you take time to think about the things that you hear? If so, you're building a stronger marriage. But if you allow the obligations of everyday living to interfere with the communications you share with your spouse, it's time to reorder your priorities.

You live in a busy world, a place where it is all too easy to overlook the needs of others, but God's Word instructs you to do otherwise. In the Gospel of Matthew, Jesus declares, "In everything, therefore, treat people the same way you want them to treat you, for this is the Law and the Prophets" (Matthew 7:12 NASB). This is the Golden Rule, and it should govern your marriage.

Do you want your voice to be heard? Of course you do. So, in adherence with the Golden Rule, you should also let your spouse's voice be heard—by you.

MORE THOUGHTS FOR TODAY

The first duty of love is to listen.

Paul Tillich

The cliché is true: People don't care what we know until they know we care.

Rick Warren

One of the best ways to encourage someone who's hurting is with you ears—by listening.

Barbara Johnson

Answering before listening is both stupid and rude.

Proverbs 18:13 MSG

OUR PRAYER FOR TODAY

Dear Lord, let us listen carefully to each other and to You.
When we listen, we learn. So, today and every day,
let us strive to understand each other as we follow
in the footsteps of Your Son.
Amen

Beyond Perfectionism

Those who wait for perfect weather will never plant seeds;
those who look at every cloud will never harvest crops.
Plant early in the morning, and work until evening,
because you don't know if this or that will succeed.
They might both do well.

Ecclesiastes 11:4,6 NCV

Marriage is an exercise in patience. From time to time, even the most considerate spouse may do things that worry us, or confuse us, or anger us. Why? Because even the most considerate spouse is still an imperfect human being, capable of missteps, misdeeds, and mistakes. And it is precisely because our loved ones are human that we learn to be patient with their shortcomings (just as they, too, must be patient with ours).

Are you one of those people who demand perfection from everybody, with the possible exception of yourself? If so, it's time to reassess your expectations. God doesn't expect perfection, and neither should you.

Proverbs 19:11 makes it clear: "People with good sense restrain their anger; they earn esteem by overlooking wrongs" (NLT). So the next time you find yourself drumming your fingers while waiting for your loved one to do the right thing, take a deep breath and ask God for patience. After all, the world unfolds according to God's timetable, not yours. And your loved ones live—and grow—according to their own timetables, too. Sometimes, you must wait patiently, and that's as it should be. After all, think how patient God has been with you.

MORE THOUGHTS FOR TODAY

Because we are rooted and grounded in love, we can be relaxed and at ease, knowing that our acceptance is not based on our performance or our perfect behavior.

Joyce Meyer

A good garden may have some weeds.

Thomas Fuller

A perfectionist resists the truth that growing up in Christ is a process.

Susan Lenzkes

Teach me Your way, O LORD; I will walk in Your truth.

Psalm 86:11 NASB

OUR PRAYER FOR TODAY

Lord, this world has so many expectations of us, but today we will not seek to meet the world's expectations; we will do our best to meet Your expectations. We will make You our ultimate priority, Lord, by serving You, by praising You, by loving You, and by obeying You.

Amen

DAY 21

Courage for Today

Be strong and courageous, and do the work.
Don't be afraid or discouraged by the size of the task,
for the LORD God, my God, is with you.
He will not fail you or forsake you.

1 Chronicles 28:20 NLT

A storm rose quickly on the Sea of Galilee, and the disciples were afraid. Although they had seen Jesus perform many miracles, the disciples feared for their lives, so they turned to their Savior, and He calmed the waters and the wind.

Sometimes, we, like the disciples, feel threatened by the inevitable storms of life. And when we are fearful, we, too, can turn to Christ for courage and for comfort.

The next time you're afraid, remember that the One who calmed the wind and the waves is also your personal Savior. And remember that the ultimate battle has already been won at Calvary. We, as believers, can live courageously in the promises of our Lord . . . and we should.

MORE THOUGHTS FOR TODAY

Perhaps I am stronger than I think.

Thomas Merton

God knows that the strength that comes from wrestling with our fear will give us wings to fly.

Paula Rinehart

When once we are assured that God is good, then there can be nothing left to fear.

Hannah Whitall Smith

Therefore, being always of good courage . . . we walk by faith, not by sight.

2 Corinthians 5:6-7 NASB

OUR PRAYER FOR TODAY

Lord, sometimes, this world is a fearful place.
Yet, You have promised that You are always with us.
Because You are our protector, we are not afraid.
Today, Dear Lord, we will live courageously as we place
our trust in Your everlasting promises
and in Your everlasting love.
Amen

Obey Him

*It is the L*ORD *your God you must follow,*
and him you must revere. Keep his commands and obey him;
serve him and hold fast to him.

Deuteronomy 13:4 NIV

O bedience to God is determined, not by words, but by deeds. Talking about righteousness is easy; living righteously is far more difficult, especially in today's temptation-filled world.

Since God created Adam and Eve, we human beings have been rebelling against our Creator. Why? Because we are unwilling to trust God's Word, and we are unwilling to follow His commandments. God has given us a guidebook for righteous living called the Holy Bible. It contains thorough instructions which, if followed, lead to fulfillment, righteousness, and salvation. But, if we choose to ignore God's commandments, the results are as predictable as they are tragic.

Unless we are willing to abide by God's laws, all of our righteous proclamations ring hollow. How can we best proclaim our love for the Lord? By obeying Him. And, for further instructions, read the manual.

MORE THOUGHTS FOR TODAY

A life of obedience is not a life of following a list of do's and don'ts, but it is allowing God to be original in our lives.

Vonette Bright

There are two things we are called to do: we are to depend on His strength and be obedient to His Word. If we can't handle being dependent and obedient, we will never become the kind of people who have a heart for God.

Stuart Briscoe

The surest evidence of our love for Christ is obedience to the laws of Christ. Love is the root, obedience is the fruit.

Matthew Henry

The world and its desires pass away, but the man who does the will of God lives forever.

1 John 2:17 NIV

OUR PRAYER FOR TODAY

Heavenly Father, when we turn our thoughts away from You and Your Word, we suffer. But when we obey Your commandments—when we place our trust in You— we are secure. Let us live according to Your commandments. Direct us far from the temptations and distractions of this world. And, let us discover Your will and follow it, dear Lord, this day and always.

Amen

Best Friends

As iron sharpens iron, a friend sharpens a friend.

Proverbs 27:17 NLT

D o you want your love to last forever? If so, here's a time-tested prescription for a blissfully happy marriage: make certain that your spouse is your best friend.

Genuine friendship between a husband and wife should be treasured and nurtured. As Christians, we are commanded to love one another. The familiar words of 1 Corinthians 13:2 remind us that love and charity are among God's greatest gifts: "And though I have the gift of prophecy, and understand all mysteries, and all knowledge; and though I have all faith, so that I could remove mountains, and have not charity, I am nothing" (KJV).

Is your spouse your best friend? If so, you are immensely blessed by God—never take this gift for granted. So today, remember the important role that friendship plays in your marriage. That friendship is, after all, a glorious gift, praised by God. Give thanks for that gift and nurture it.

A true friend is the gift of God.

Robert South

MORE THOUGHTS FOR TODAY

Whether you are blessed with soulmates, or with those who walk with you just a little while, not a single one of these friends crosses your path by chance. Each is a messenger, sent by God, to give you the wisdom, companionship, comfort, or challenge you need for a particular leg of your spiritual journey.

Traci Mullins

The thread of our life would be dark, Heaven knows! If it were not with friendship and love intertwin'd.

St. Thomas More

Beloved, if God so loved us, we also ought to love one another.

1 John 4:11 NKJV

OUR PRAYER FOR TODAY

Dear Lord, today and every day, let our marriage be
a celebration of love, respect, consideration,
obedience, and friendship.
Amen

Beyond Anger

When you are angry, do not sin, and be sure to stop being
angry before the end of the day.
Do not give the devil a way to defeat you.

Ephesians 4:26–27 NCV

Anger is a natural human emotion that is sometimes necessary and appropriate. Even Jesus became angry when confronted with the moneychangers in the temple (Matthew 21:12). Righteous indignation is an appropriate response to evil, but God does not intend that anger should rule our lives. And, just as importantly, God does not intend that anger should rule our marriages. He instructs us to turn away from anger whenever possible and forgive others just as we seek forgiveness for ourselves. And forgiveness, like so many other things, starts at home.

Life is full of frustrations: some great and some small. Most of our frustrations are of the more mundane variety. As long as we live, we will inevitably face countless opportunities to lose our tempers over small, relatively insignificant events: a traffic jam, a spilled cup of coffee, an inconsiderate comment, a forgotten promise.

When you are tempted to lose your temper over the minor inconveniences of life, don't. And while you're at it, don't bring anger into the sanctity of your marriage. Turn away from anger and turn instead to God. When you do, you'll honor Him by sharing His gift: the gift of peace. And what a beautiful gift it is.

MORE THOUGHTS FOR TODAY

Get rid of the poison of built-up anger and the acid of long-term resentment.

Charles Swindoll

Anger unresolved will only bring you woe.

Kay Arthur

There is no sin nor wrong that gives a man such a foretaste of hell in this life as anger and impatience.

St. Catherine of Siena

Everyone should be quick to listen, slow to speak and slow to become angry, for man's anger does not bring about the righteous life that God desires.

James 1:19-20 NIV

OUR PRAYER FOR TODAY

Lord, sometimes, in moments of frustration,
we become angry. When we fall prey to irrational anger,
give us inner calm. Let us show our thankfulness to You
by offering forgiveness to each other. And, when we do,
let others see Your love reflected through
our words and our deeds.
Amen

Giving More

A new commandment I give to you,
that you love one another; as I have loved you,
that you also love one another.

John 13:34 NKJV

When it comes to your marriage, who's Number One: you or your spouse? If you consistently place your own needs above the needs of your loved one, you're probably headed for trouble, and fast.

Jesus taught that the most esteemed men and women are not those who say "me first." Christ instructed us that the greatest among us will be "servants of all" (Mark 9:35). And these words are especially true in the context of marriage.

Are you willing to contribute unselfishly to the wellbeing of your loved one? And are you willing to do so without constantly comparing your own good deeds to the deeds of your spouse? If so, your marriage will be blessed by your unselfishness. If not, it's time to heed this word of advice: The best way to make love last is by saying "you first"—and meaning it.

MORE THOUGHTS FOR TODAY

It's not difficult to make an impact on your world. All you really have to do is put the needs of others ahead of your own. You can make a difference with a little time and a big heart.

James Dobson

Love is an attribute of God. To love others is evidence of a genuine faith.

Kay Arthur

When you taste a measure of being able to love and enjoy the people in your life, without having to have any particular response from them, you are tasting bliss.

Paula Rinehart

Honor all people. Love the brotherhood. Fear God. Honor the king.

1 Peter 2:17 NKJV

OUR PRAYER FOR TODAY

Father, help me always to treat others as I wish to be treated. Let me be kind, fair, and respectful. Let me rejoice in the victories of others, and let me be understanding when others fall short. In all my dealings, let me be guided by the example of Christ so that I might glorify Your Son through my words, my deeds, my love for others.

Amen

Embracing Your Future

What a God we have! And how fortunate we are to have him,
this Father of our Master Jesus! Because Jesus was raised
from the dead, we've been given a brand-new life
and have everything to live for, including a future in heaven—
and the future starts now!

1 Peter 1:3-4 MSG

Sometimes the future seems bright, and sometimes it does not. Yet even when we cannot see the possibilities of tomorrow, God can. Our challenge is to trust ourselves to do the best work we can, and then to trust God to do the rest.

When we trust God, we should trust Him without reservation. We should steel ourselves against the inevitable disappointments of the day, secure in the knowledge that our Heavenly Father has a plan for the future that is brighter than we can imagine.

Are you willing to look to the future with trust and confidence? Hopefully so, because the future should not be feared, it should be embraced. And it most certainly should be embraced by you.

MORE THOUGHTS FOR TODAY

The future is as bright as the promises of God.

Adoniram Judson

The Christian believes in a fabulous future.

Billy Graham

Never be afraid to trust an unknown future to a known God.

Corrie ten Boom

I say this because I know what I am planning for you," says the Lord. "I have good plans for you, not plans to hurt you. I will give you hope and a good future."

Jeremiah 29:11 NCV

OUR PRAYER FOR TODAY

Lord, sometimes life is so difficult that the future seems
foreboding. And sometimes we may lose hope.
But with You, there is always hope. Today, we will keep
Your promises in our hearts, and we will trust
the future to You.
Amen

Genuine Peace

I leave you peace; my peace I give you.
I do not give it to you as the world does.
So don't let your hearts be troubled or afraid.

John 14:27 NCV

Peace with God. Peace with self. Peace with others. Do you possess that kind of peace? Have you found the genuine peace that can be yours through Jesus Christ, or are you still rushing after the illusion of "peace and happiness" that the world promises but cannot deliver? The words of John 14:27 remind us that Jesus offers us peace, not as the world gives, but as He alone gives. Our challenge is to accept Christ's peace into our hearts and then, as best we can, to share His peace with our neighbors.

Today, as a gift to yourself, to your family, and to your friends, claim the inner peace that is your spiritual birthright: the peace of Jesus Christ. It is offered freely; it has been paid for in full; it is yours for the asking. So ask. And then share.

"My peace I give unto you"; it is a peace all over from the crown of the head to the sole of the feet, an irrepressible confidence.

Oswald Chambers

MORE THOUGHTS FOR TODAY

God is in control of history; it's His story. Doesn't that give you a great peace—especially when world events seems so tumultuous and insane?

Kay Arthur

We need to be at peace with our past, content with our present, and sure about our future, knowing they are all in God's hands.

Joyce Meyer

If your sinful nature controls your mind, there is death. But if the Holy Spirit controls your mind, there is life and peace.

Romans 8:6 NLT

OUR PRAYER FOR TODAY

Dear Lord, let us accept the peace and abundance that You offer through Your Son Jesus. You are the Giver of all things good, Father, and You give us peace when we draw close to You. Help us to trust Your will, to follow Your commands, and to accept Your peace, today and forever.
Amen

Beyond Bitterness

All bitterness, anger and wrath, insult and slander must be removed from you, along with all wickedness. And be kind and compassionate to one another, forgiving one another, just as God also forgave you in Christ.

Ephesians 4:31-32 Holman CSB

Bitterness is a spiritual sickness. It will consume your soul; it is dangerous to your emotional health. It can destroy you if you let it . . . so don't let it!

If you are caught up in intense feelings of anger or resentment, you know all too well the destructive power of these emotions. How can you rid yourself of these feelings? First, you must prayerfully ask God to cleanse your heart. Then, you must learn to catch yourself whenever thoughts of bitterness or hatred begin to attack you. Your challenge is this: You must learn to resist negative thoughts before they hijack your emotions.

Matthew 5:22 teaches us that if we judge our brothers and sisters, we, too, will be subject to judgement. Let us refrain, then, from judging our neighbors. Instead, let us forgive them and love them, while leaving their judgement to a far more capable authority: the One who sits on His throne in heaven.

MORE THOUGHTS FOR TODAY

Bitterness is the greatest barrier to friendship with God.

Rick Warren

Bitterness is the trap that snares the hunter.

Max Lucado

By not forgiving, by not letting wrongs go, we aren't getting back at anyone. We are merely punishing ourselves by barricading our own hearts.

Jim Cymbala

Do not repay anyone evil for evil. Try to do what is honorable in everyone's eyes.

Romans 12:17 Holman CSB

OUR PRAYER FOR TODAY

Heavenly Father, free us from anger and bitterness.
When we are angry, we cannot feel Your peace.
When we are bitter, we cannot sense Your presence.
Let us turn away from bitterness and regret as we claim
the spiritual abundance that You offer through
the gift of Your Son.
Amen

Praise Him

Is anyone happy? Let him sing songs of praise.

James 5:13 NIV

It's easy to "compartmentalize" our waking hours into a few familiar categories: work, rest, play, family time, and worship. As creatures of habit, we may find ourselves praising God only at particular times of the day or on a particular day of the week. But praise for our Creator should never be reserved for mealtimes, or bedtimes, or church. Instead, we should praise God all day, every day, to the greatest extent we can, with thanksgiving in our hearts, and with a song on our lips.

Worship and praise should be woven into the fabric of everything we do; they should not be relegated to a weekly three-hour visit to church on Sunday morning. A. W. Tozer correctly observed, "If you will not worship God seven days a week, you do not worship Him on one day a week."

Do you and your spouse praise God many times each day? If so, keep up the good work; if not, it's time to reassess your priorities. When you consider the wonderful things that God has done for you, you'll find the time—or more accurately you'll make the time—to praise Him for all that He has done.

Every time you notice a gift from the Creator, thank Him and praise Him. His works are marvelous, His gifts are beyond understanding, and His love endures forever.

MORE THOUGHTS FOR TODAY

I am to praise God for all things, regardless of where they seem to originate. Doing this is the key to receiving the blessings of God. Praise will wash away my resentments.

Catherine Marshall

Worship is an act which develops feelings for God, not a feeling for God which is expressed in an act of worship. When we obey the command to praise God in worship, our deep, essential need to be in relationship with God is nurtured.

Eugene Peterson

Praise Him! Praise Him! Tell of His excellent greatness. Praise Him! Praise Him! Ever in joyful song!

Fanny Crosby

Through Him then, let us continually offer up a sacrifice of praise to God, that is, the fruit of lips that give thanks to His name.

Hebrews 13:15 NASB

OUR PRAYER FOR TODAY

Dear Lord, today and every day we will praise You.
We will come to You with hope in our hearts and words of gratitude on our lips. Let our thoughts, our prayers, our words, and our deeds praise You now and forever.
Amen

The Power of Prayer

"Relax, Daniel," he continued, "don't be afraid.
From the moment you decided to humble yourself
to receive understanding, your prayer was heard,
and I set out to come to you."

Daniel 10:12 MSG

I s prayer an integral part of your married life or is it a hit-or-miss habit? Do you and your spouse "pray without ceasing," or is prayer usually an afterthought? Do you regularly pray together, or do you only bow your heads in unison during Sunday morning services? The answer to these questions determine the quality of your prayer life and, to a surprising extent, the spiritual strength of your marriage.

Andrew Murray observed, "Some people pray just to pray, and some people pray to know God." Your task, along with your spouse, is to pray together, not out of habit or obligation, but out of a sincere desire to know God.

Through constant prayers, you and your spouse should petition God, you should praise God, and you should seek God's guidance for your marriage and your life.

Prayer changes things, prayer changes people, and prayer changes marriages. So don't limit your prayers to meals or to bedtime. Pray constantly about things great and small. God is listening, and He wants to hear from you—and your spouse—right now.

MORE THOUGHTS FOR TODAY

I have witnessed many attitudes make a positive turnaround through prayer.

John Maxwell

Throughout history, the presence and the power of prayer in the lives of righteous men and women has born testimony to the dependence of mankind on a benevolent, caring God.

Jim Gallery

If you don't know what you're doing, pray to the Father. He loves to help. You'll get his help, and won't be condescended to when you ask for it. Ask boldly, believingly, without a second thought. People who "worry their prayers" are like wind-whipped waves. Don't think you're going to get anything from the Master that way, adrift at sea, keeping all your options open.

James 1:5-8 MSG

OUR PRAYER FOR TODAY

We pray to You, Father, because You desire it and because we need it. Prayer not only changes things, it changes us. Help us, Lord, never to face the demands of the day without first spending time with You.

Amen

Problem-solving 101

Let not your heart be troubled: ye believe in God,
believe also in me.

John 14:1 KJV

From time to time, all of us face problems, disappointments, heartaches, and loss. Old Man Trouble pays periodic visits to each of us; none of us are exempt, and neither are our marriages. When we are troubled, God stands ready and willing to protect us. Our responsibility, of course, is to ask for His healing touch. When we call upon Him in heartfelt prayer, He will answer—in His own time and in accordance with His own perfect plan.

When we encounter problems or misunderstandings in our relationships, we must work to heal those problems sooner rather than later. Marital problems, like all problems, are most easily solved when they are new and small. That's why wise couples do the hard work of addressing their problems honestly, forthrightly, and quickly (even when they might prefer to downplay their difficulties or ignore those difficulties altogether).

Ignoring problems instead of fixing them is tempting but irresponsible. After all, if we won't solve our problems, who will? Or should?

In summary, the hallmark of a healthy marriage is not the absence of problems, but a willingness to solve those problems now. May you live—and love—accordingly.

MORE THOUGHTS FOR TODAY

Often, in the midst of great problems, we stop short of the real blessing God has for us, which is a fresh vision of who He is.

Anne Graham Lotz

Winners see an answer for every problem; losers see a problem in every answer.

Barbara Johnson

We are all faced with a series of great opportunities, brilliantly disguised as unsolvable problems. Unsolvable without God's wisdom, that is.

Charles Swindoll

People who do what is right may have many problems, but the Lord will solve them all.

Psalm 34:19 NCV

OUR PRAYER FOR TODAY

Lord, sometimes our problems are simply too big for us, but they are never too big for You. We will turn our troubles over to You, Lord, and we will trust You today and for all eternity.
Amen

DAY 32

Seeking God's Approval

For the eyes of the Lord are over the righteous,
and his ears are open unto their prayers:
but the face of the Lord is against them that do evil.

1 Peter 3:12 KJV

As Christians, we are called to walk with God and obey His commandments. When we seek righteousness in our own lives—and when we enjoy the companionship of those who do likewise—we reap the spiritual rewards that God has promised us. When we behave ourselves as godly men and women, when we live righteously and according to God's commandments, He blesses us in ways that we cannot fully understand.

Would you like a time-tested formula for a successful marriage and a successful life? Here is a formula that is proven and true: Seek God's approval in every aspect of your life. Does this sound too simple? Perhaps it is simple, but it is also the only way to reap the marvelous riches that God has in store for you.

So today, take every step of your journey with God as your traveling companion. Read His Word and follow His commandments. Support only those activities that further God's kingdom and your spiritual growth. Be an example of righteousness to your spouse, to your neighbors, and to your children. Then, reap the blessings that God has promised to all those who live according to His will and His Word.

MORE THOUGHTS FOR TODAY

The soul of a righteous person is nothing but a paradise, in which, as God tells us, He takes His delight.

St. Teresa of Avila

Trusting God is the bottom line of Christian righteousness.

R. C. Sproul

A man who lives right, and is right, has more power in his silence than another has by his words.

Phillips Brooks

Blessed are the pure of heart, for they will see God.

Matthew 5:8 NIV

OUR PRAYER FOR TODAY

Dear Lord, this world is filled with so many temptations, distractions, and frustrations. When we turn our thoughts away from You and Your Word, we suffer.
But when we turn our thoughts and prayers toward You and Your Son, we are secure. Direct us, Father, today and every day that we live.
Amen

Enthusiasm Now

Whatever you do, do it enthusiastically,
as something done for the Lord and not for men.

Colossians 3:23 Holman CSB

D o you see each day as a glorious opportunity to serve God and to do His will? Are you enthused about life, or do you struggle through each day giving scarcely a thought to God's blessings? Are you constantly praising God for His gifts, and are you sharing His Good News with the world? And are you excited about the possibilities for service that God has placed before you, whether at home, at work, at church, or at school? You should be.

You are the recipient of Christ's sacrificial love. Accept it enthusiastically and share it fervently. Jesus deserves your enthusiasm; the world deserves it; and you deserve the experience of sharing it.

When we wholeheartedly commit ourselves to God, there is nothing mediocre or run-of-the-mill about us. To live for Christ is to be passionate about our Lord and about our lives.

Jim Gallery

MORE THOUGHTS FOR TODAY

It is a remarkable thing that some of the most optimistic and enthusiastic people you will meet are those who have been through intense suffering.

Warren Wiersbe

Your enthusiasm will be infectious, stimulating, and attractive to others. They will love you for it. They will go for you and with you.

Norman Vincent Peale

Never be lazy in your work, but serve the Lord enthusiastically.
Romans 12:11 NLT

OUR PRAYER FOR TODAY

Dear Lord, You have promised that we can experience abundance and joy. Today and every day, we will strive to maintain our passion for life—and our passion for You. We will be enthusiastic followers of Your Son, and we will share His Good News—and His love— with all those who cross our paths.
Amen

The Golden Rule for Couples

Let us not become weary in doing good,
for at the proper time we will reap a harvest
if we do not give up.

Galatians 6:9 NIV

Is the Golden Rule one of the rules that governs your household? Hopefully so. Obeying the Golden Rule is a proven way to improve any relationship, including your marriage. But the reverse is also true: if you or your spouse ignore the Golden Rule altogether, you're headed for trouble, and fast.

Too many marriages become unbalanced when one partner assumes the role of the "taker" while the other partner accepts the role of the "giver." But the healthiest marriages are those in which both parties seek to give more than they get.

Jesus made Himself perfectly clear: He instructed us to treat others in the same way that we want to be treated. That means that we must treat other people (including our loved ones) with respect, kindness, and courtesy.

So if you're wondering how you should treat your spouse (or anyone else, for that matter), ask the person you see every time you look into the mirror. The answer you receive will tell you exactly what to do.

MORE THOUGHTS FOR TODAY

It is wrong for anyone to be anxious to receive more from his neighbor than he himself is willing to give to God.

St. Francis of Assisi

The Golden Rule starts at home, but it should never stop there.

Marie T. Freeman

It is one of the most beautiful compensations of life that no one can sincerely try to help another without helping herself.

Barbara Johnson

Each of you should look not only to your own interests, but also to the interest of others.

Philippians 2:4 NIV

OUR PRAYER FOR TODAY

Dear Lord, we thank You for friends and family members who practice the Golden Rule. Because we expect to be treated with kindness, let us be kind. Because we wish to be loved, let us be loving. Because we need forgiveness, let us be merciful. In matters great and small, let us live by the Golden Rule, and let us express our gratitude to those who offer kindness and generosity to us.

Amen

A High Priority?

You will be a good servant of Christ Jesus,
constantly nourished on the words of the faith
and of the sound doctrine which you have been following.

1 Timothy 4:6 NASB

I s Bible study a high priority for you and your family? The answer to this simple question will determine, to a surprising extent, the quality of your lives and the direction of your faith.

As a family, you must decide whether God's Word will be a bright spotlight that guides your path every day or a tiny nightlight that occasionally flickers in the dark. The decision to study the Bible—or not—is yours individually and collectively. But make no mistake: how your family chooses to use the Bible will have a profound impact on every member of the household.

George Mueller observed, "The vigor of our spiritual lives will be in exact proportion to the place held by the Bible in our lives and in our thoughts." Think of it like this: the more you use your Bible, the more God uses you.

Perhaps your bookshelf is filled with Bibles that are read infrequently. If so, remember the old saying, "A Bible in the hand is worth two in the bookcase." Or perhaps yours is one of those families that is simply "too busy" to find time for a daily dose of prayer and Bible study. If so, remember the old adage, "It's hard to stumble when you're on your knees."

God's Word can be a roadmap to a place of righteous and abundance. Make it your family's roadmap. God's wisdom can be a light to guide your steps. Claim it as your family's light today, tomorrow, and every day of your life— and then walk confidently in the footsteps of God's only begotten Son.

MORE THOUGHTS FOR TODAY

Since the Christian's Point of Reference is the Bible, it's a happy couple who look there for guidance.

Ruth Bell Graham

Reading news without reading the Bible will inevitably lead to an unbalanced life, an anxious spirit, a worried and depressed soul.

Bill Bright

But grow in the grace and knowledge of our Lord and Savior Jesus Christ. To Him be the glory both now and forever. Amen.

2 Peter 3:18 NKJV

OUR PRAYER FOR TODAY

Father, Your Holy Word is a light unto the world; we will study it, trust it, and share it. In all that we do, help us be worthy witnesses for You as we share the Good News of Your perfect Son and Your perfect Word.

Amen

The Firm Foundation

Unfailing love surrounds those who trust the LORD.

Psalm 32:10 NLT

God loves you. Period. He loves you more than you can imagine; His affection is deeper and more profound than you can fathom. God made you in His own image and gave you salvation through the person of His Son Jesus Christ. And now, precisely because you are a wondrous creation treasured by God, a crucial question presents itself: What will you do in response to God's love? Will you ignore it or embrace it? Will you return it or neglect it? Will you deny it, or will you share it? These decisions, of course, are yours and yours alone.

When you embrace God's love, you are forever changed. When you embrace God's love, you feel differently about yourself, your loved ones, your marriage, and your world. When you embrace God's love, you share His message—and His mercy—with others.

Have you built every aspect of your life—including your marriage—upon the firm foundation of God's unwavering love for you and yours? If so, you have built your life on the Rock that cannot be moved. And, you have accepted a priceless gift that is yours to share and to keep . . . now and throughout all eternity.

MORE THOUGHTS FOR TODAY

God has the marvelous ability to love us in the midst of our imperfections.

Joyce Meyer

We can all humbly say in the sincerity of faith, "I am loved; I am called; I am secure."

Franklin Graham

God is every moment totally aware of each one of us. Totally aware in intense concentration and love. No one passes through any area of life, happy or tragic, without the attention of God with him.

Eugenia Price

But God demonstrates His own love toward us, in that while we were still sinners, Christ died for us.

Romans 5:8 NKJV

OUR PRAYER FOR TODAY

God, You are love. Today and every day, we will return Your love . . . and we will share it. We will strive to be loving, faithful servants to You and to Your Son, this day and throughout eternity.

Amen

The Ultimate Protection

*I know whom I have believed and am persuaded that He is able
to guard what has been entrusted to me until that day.*

2 Timothy 1:12 Holman CSB

The hand of God encircles us and comforts us in times of adversity. In times of hardship, He restores our strength; in times of sorrow, He dries our tears. When we are troubled, or weak, or embittered, God is as near as our next breath.

God has promised to protect us, and He intends to fulfill His promise. In a world filled with dangers and temptations, God is the ultimate armor. In a world filled with misleading messages, God's Word is the ultimate truth. In a world filled with more frustrations than we can count, God's Son offers the ultimate peace.

Will you accept God's peace and wear God's armor against the dangers of our world? Hopefully so, because when you do, you can live courageously, knowing that you possess the ultimate protection: God's unfailing love for you.

MORE THOUGHTS FOR TODAY

The Rock of Ages is the great sheltering encirclement.

Oswald Chambers

Prayer is our pathway not only to divine protection, but also to a personal, intimate relationship with God.

Shirley Dobson

Through the storm, through the night. Lead me on to the light. Take my hand precious Lord, lead me home.

Thomas A. Dorsey

The Lord is my rock, my fortress, and my deliverer.

Psalm 18:2 Holman CSB

OUR PRAYER FOR TODAY

Lord, You are our Shepherd. You care for us;
You comfort us; You watch over us; and You have saved us.
We will praise You, Father, for Your glorious works, for
Your protection, for Your love, and for Your Son.
Amen

He Is Sufficient

The LORD is my strength and song,
and He has become my salvation.

Exodus 15:2 NASB

It is easy to become overwhelmed by the demands of everyday life, but if you're a faithful follower of the One from Galilee, you need never be overwhelmed. Why? Because God's love is sufficient to meet your needs. Whatever dangers you may face, whatever heartbreaks you must endure, God is with you, and He stands ready to comfort you and to heal you.

The Psalmist writes, "Weeping may endure for a night, but joy comes in the morning" (Psalm 30:5 NKJV). But when we are suffering, the morning may seem very far away. It is not. God promises that He is "near to those who have a broken heart" (Psalm 34:18 NKJV).

If you are experiencing the intense pain of a recent loss, or if you are still mourning a loss from long ago, perhaps you are now ready to begin the next stage of your journey with God. If so, be mindful of this fact: the loving heart of God is sufficient to meet any challenge, including yours.

MORE THOUGHTS FOR TODAY

God is always sufficient in perfect proportion to our need.

Beth Moore

God is, must be, our answer to every question and every cry of need.

Hannah Whitall Smith

I grew up learning to be self-reliant, but now, to grow up in Christ, I must unlearn self-reliance and learn self-distrust in light of his all-sufficiency.

Mary Morrison Suggs

Finally, my brethren, be strong in the Lord and in the power of His might. Put on the whole armor of God, that you may be able to stand against the wiles of the devil.

Ephesians 6:10-11 NKJV

OUR PRAYER FOR TODAY

Dear Lord, whatever "it" is, You can handle it!
Let us turn to You when we are fearful or worried.
You are our loving Heavenly Father; You are sufficient in
all things; and we trust You always.
Amen

A Passion for Life

He did it with all his heart. So he prospered.

2 Chronicles 31:21 NKJV

Are you and your spouse passionate about your life, your loved ones, your work, your marriage, and your Savior? You should be. As thoughtful Christians, you have every reason to live passionately, but sometimes the struggles of everyday living may leave you feeling discouraged, or exhausted, or both.

If you fear that your spouse's passion for life is slowly fading away, it's time to slow down, to rest, to recount your blessings, to worship, and to pray. When you feel worried or weary, you must pray fervently for God to renew your sense of wonderment and excitement.

Our world desperately needs faithful believers who are passionate about their lives and their faith. Be such a believer. The world desperately needs your enthusiasm, and just as importantly, you need the experience of sharing it.

When you allow Christ to reign over your heart— when you worship Him with words, thoughts, prayers, and deeds—your life can become a glorious adventure. When you live passionately—and share your passion with others—God will most certainly bless you and yours . . . today and forever.

MORE THOUGHTS FOR TODAY

Let us live with urgency. Let us exploit the opportunity of life. Let us not drift. Let us live intentionally. We must not trifle our lives away.

Raymond Ortlund

Get absolutely enthralled with something. Throw yourself into it with abandon. Get out of yourself. Be somebody. Do something.

Norman Vincent Peale

One can never consent to creep when one feels an impulse to soar.

Helen Keller

Do not lack diligence; be fervent in spirit; serve the Lord.
Romans 12:11 Holman CSB

OUR PRAYER FOR TODAY

Dear Lord, we thank You for Your countless blessings.
We will demonstrate our gratitude by living obediently
and passionately. We praise You, Father,
for Your blessings, for Your love, and for Your Son.
Amen

DAY 40

The Blame Game

Walking down the street, Jesus saw a man blind from birth.
His disciples asked, "Rabbi, who sinned: this man or his
parents, causing him to be born blind?" Jesus said,
"You're asking the wrong question. You're looking for someone
to blame. There is no such cause-effect here.
Look instead for what God can do."

John 9:1-3 MSG

To blame others for our own problems is the height of futility. Yet blaming others is a favorite human pastime. Why? Because blaming is much easier than fixing, and criticizing others is so much easier than improving ourselves. So instead of solving our problems legitimately (by doing the work required to solve them) we are inclined to fret, to blame, and to criticize, while doing precious little else. When we do, our problems, quite predictably, remain unsolved.

Have you acquired the bad habit of blaming others for problems that you could or should solve yourself? If so, you are not only disobeying God's Word, you are also wasting your own precious time. So, instead of looking for someone to blame, look for something to fix, and then get busy fixing it. And as you consider your own situation, remember this: God has a way of helping those who help themselves, but He doesn't spend much time helping those who don't.

MORE THOUGHTS FOR TODAY

The main thing is this: we should never blame anyone or anything for our defeats. No matter how evil their intentions may be, they are altogether unable to harm us until we begin to blame them and use them as excuses for our own unbelief.

A. W. Tozer

You'll never win the blame game, so why even bother to play?

Marie T. Freeman

Instead of looking for someone to blame, look for something to fix, and then get busy fixing it.

Jim Gallery

People's own foolishness ruins their lives, but in their minds they blame the Lord.

Proverbs 19:3 NCV

OUR PRAYER FOR TODAY

Dear Lord, free us from the poison of bitterness and the futility of blame. Let us turn away from destructive emotions so that we may know the perfect peace and spiritual abundance that can be ours through You.

Amen

DAY 41

Beyond Materialism

Do not love the world or the things in the world.
If anyone loves the world, the love of the Father is not in him.
1 John 2:15 NKJV

Earthly riches are temporary. Spiritual riches, on the other hand, are everlasting. Yet all too often, we focus our thoughts and energies on the accumulation of earthly treasures, leaving precious little time for anything else.

Far too many marriages are weighted down by endless concerns about money and possessions. Too many couples mistakenly focus their thoughts and efforts on newer cars, better clothes, and bigger houses. The results of these misplaced priorities are always unfortunate, and sometimes tragic.

Certainly we all need the basic necessities of life, but once we meet those needs for our families and ourselves, the piling up of possessions creates more problems than it solves. Our real riches are not of this world: we are never really rich until we are rich in spirit.

Do you find yourself wrapped up in the concerns of the material world? If so, it's time for you and your spouse to sit down and have a heart-to-heart talk about "stuff." When you do, you should reorder your priorities by turning away from materialism and back to God. Then, you can begin storing up riches that will endure throughout eternity: the spiritual kind.

MORE THOUGHTS FOR TODAY

As faithful stewards of what we have, ought we not to give earnest thought to our staggering surplus?

Elisabeth Elliot

The cross is laid on every Christian. It begins with the call to abandon the attachments of this world.

Dietrich Bonhoeffer

The socially prescribed affluent, middle-class lifestyle has become so normative in our churches that we discern little conflict between it and the Christian lifestyle prescribed in the New Testament.

Tony Campolo

He who trusts in his riches will fall, but the righteous will flourish. . . .

Proverbs 11:28 NKJV

OUR PRAYER FOR TODAY

Heavenly Father, when we focus intently upon You,
we are blessed. When we focus too intently on
the acquisition of material possessions, we are troubled.
Make our priorities pleasing to You, Father,
and make us worthy servants of Your Son.
Amen

Counting God's Blessings

For surely, O LORD, you bless the righteous;
you surround them with your favor as with a shield.

Psalm 5:12 NIV

If you sat down and began counting your blessings, how long would it take? A very, very long time! Your blessings include life, freedom, family, friends, talents, and possessions, for starters. But, your greatest blessing—a gift that is yours for the asking—is God's gift of salvation through Christ Jesus.

Today, give thanks for your blessings by accepting them fully (with open arms) and by sharing them generously (with a thankful heart).

Billy Graham had this advice: "Think of the blessings we so easily take for granted: Life itself; preservation from danger; every bit of health we enjoy; every hour of liberty; the ability to see, to hear, to speak, to think, and to imagine all this comes from the hand of God." And that's sound advice for Christians—like you—who have been blessed beyond measure.

MORE THOUGHTS FOR TODAY

The Christian life is motivated, not by a list of do's and don'ts, but by the gracious outpouring of God's love and blessing.

Anne Graham Lotz

Grace is an outrageous blessing bestowed freely on a totally undeserving recipient.

Bill Hybels

God is always far more willing to give us good things than we are anxious to have them.

Catherine Marshall

I will bless them and the places surrounding my hill. I will send down showers in season; there will be showers of blessings.

Ezekiel 34:26 NIV

OUR PRAYER FOR TODAY

Dear Lord, You have given us so much, and we are thankful. We know that every good gift is to be shared with others. We give thanks for Your gifts . . . and we will share them.

Amen

Character Counts

Do not be misled: "Bad company corrupts good character."

1 Corinthians 15:33 NIV

Beth Moore correctly observed, "Those who walk in truth walk in liberty." Godly men and women agree. As believers in Christ, we must seek to live each day with discipline, honesty, and faith. When we do, at least two things happen: integrity becomes a habit, and God blesses us because of our obedience to Him. Living a life of integrity isn't always the easiest way, but it is always the right way . . . and God clearly intends that it should be our way, too.

Character isn't built overnight; it is built slowly over a lifetime. It is the sum of every sensible choice, every honorable decision, and every honest word. It is forged on the anvil of sincerity and polished by the virtue of fairness. Character is a precious thing—preserve yours at all costs.

It is the thoughts and intents of the heart that shape a person's life.

John Eldredge

MORE THOUGHTS FOR TODAY

No man can use his Bible with power unless he has the character of Jesus in his heart.

Alan Redpath

Often, our character is at greater risk in prosperity than in adversity.

Beth Moore

Your true character is something that no one can injure but yourself.

C. H. Spurgeon

Applying all diligence, in your faith supply moral excellence.
2 Peter 1:5 NASB

OUR PRAYER FOR TODAY

Lord, You know us far better than we know ourselves. Today, we will strive to serve You and to obey Your commandments. Let our words and deeds be pleasing to You this day and every day.
Amen

So Many Choices

I am offering you life or death, blessings or curses.
Now, choose life! . . . To choose life is to love the Lord your
God, obey him, and stay close to him.

Deuteronomy 30:19-20 NCV

Because we are creatures of free will, we make choices—lots of them. When we make choices that are pleasing to our Heavenly Father, we are blessed. When we make choices that cause us to walk in the footsteps of God's Son, we enjoy the abundance that Christ has promised to those who follow Him. But when we make choices that are displeasing to God, we sow seeds that have the potential to bring forth a bitter harvest.

Today, as you encounter the challenges of everyday living, you will make hundreds of choices. Choose wisely. Make your thoughts and your actions pleasing to God. And remember: every choice that is displeasing to Him is the wrong choice—no exceptions.

Faith is not a feeling; it is action. It is a willed choice.

Elisabeth Elliot

MORE THOUGHTS FOR TODAY

I believe with all my heart and soul that at every important crossroads in my life I was faced with a choice: between right and wrong, between serving God and pleasing myself. I didn't always make the right choice. In fact, I stumbled down the wrong path more times than I marched down the right one. But God heard the earnest prayers of those who loved me and by His grace brought me to my knees.

Al Green

Life is pretty much like a cafeteria line—it offers us many choices, both good and bad. The Christian must have a spiritual radar that detects the difference not only between bad and good but also among good, better, and best.

Dennis Swanberg

But Daniel purposed in his heart that he would not defile himself. . . .

Daniel 1:8 KJV

OUR PRAYER FOR TODAY

Dear Lord, help us to make choices that are pleasing to
You. Help us to be honest, patient, and kind.
And above all, help us to follow the teachings of Jesus,
not just today, but every day.
Amen

Look to Christ

Therefore if any man be in Christ, he is a new creature:
old things are passed away; behold, all things are become new.
2 Corinthians 5:17 KJV

Hannah Whitall Smith spoke to believers of every generation when she advised, "Keep your face upturned to Christ as the flowers do to the sun. Look, and your soul shall live and grow." How true. When we turn our hearts to Jesus, we receive His blessings, His peace, and His grace.

Christ is the ultimate Savior of mankind and the personal Savior of those who believe in Him. As His servants, we should place Him at the very center of our lives. And, every day that God gives us breath, we should share Christ's love and His message with a world that needs both.

The cross means this: Jesus taking our place to satisfy the demands of God's justice and turning aside God's wrath.
James Montgomery Boice

MORE THOUGHTS FOR TODAY

Just as I am, without one plea, but that thy blood was shed for me, and that thou bidst me come to thee, O Lamb of God, I come, I come. Just as I am, and waiting not to rid my soul of one dark blot, to thee whose blood can cleanse each spot, O Lamb of God, I come, I come.

Charlotte Elliott

If a husband and wife are deeply committed to Jesus Christ, they enjoy enormous advantages over the family with no spiritual dimension.

James Dobson

For the Son of man is come to save that which was lost.
Matthew 18:11 KJV

OUR PRAYER FOR TODAY

Dear Jesus, we are humbled by Your love and mercy.
You went to Calvary so that we might have eternal life.
Thank You, Jesus, for Your priceless gift, and for Your love.
You loved us first, Lord, and we will return
Your love today and forever.
Amen

His Power

*For His divine power has given us everything required for life
and godliness, through the knowledge of Him who called us
by His own glory and goodness.*

2 Peter 1:3 Holman CSB

When you invite Christ to rule over your heart, you avail yourself of His power. And make no mistake about it: You and Christ, working together, can do miraculous things. In fact, miraculous things are exactly what Christ intends for you to do, but He won't force you to do great things on His behalf. The decision to become a full-fledged participant in His power is a decision that you must make for yourself.

The words of John 14:12 make this promise: when you put absolute faith in Christ, you can share in His power. Today, trust the Savior's promise and expect a miracle in His name.

The Christian life is not simply following principles but being empowered to fulfill our purpose: knowing and exalting Christ.

Franklin Graham

MORE THOUGHTS FOR TODAY

Look at Christ. He rides not upon a horse which is a steed of war. He comes not with appalling pomp and power but sits upon a donkey, which is a gentle beast to bear burdens and work for men. From this we see that Christ comes not to terrify, to drive, and to oppress, but instead to help and to take for Himself our load.

Martin Luther

I now know the power of the risen Lord! He lives! The dawn of Easter has broken in my own soul! My night is gone!

Mrs. Charles E. Cowman

I pray also that you will have greater understanding in your heart so you will know the hope to which he has called us and that you will know how rich and glorious are the blessings God has promised his holy people. And you will know that God's power is very great for us who believe.

Ephesians 1:18-19 NCV

OUR PRAYER FOR TODAY

Dear Lord, Your Son died for the salvation of all mankind,
and He died for us. Through the power of Christ,
we can be compassionate, courageous, and strong.
Help us to use that power, Father, for the glory of
Your kingdom, today and forever.
Amen

Always Humble

Finally, all of you should be of one mind,
full of sympathy toward each other, loving one another
with tender hearts and humble minds.

1 Peter 3:8 NLT

G od's Word clearly instructs us to be humble. And that's good because, as fallible human beings, we have so very much to be humble about! Yet some of us continue to puff ourselves up, seeming to say, "Look at me!" To do so is wrong.

As Christians, we have been refashioned and saved by Jesus Christ, and that salvation came not because of our own good works but because of God's grace. How, then, can we be prideful? The answer, of course, is that, if we are honest with ourselves and with our God, we simply can't be boastful…we must, instead, be eternally grateful and exceedingly humble.

Are you exceedingly humble in every aspect of your life, including your relationships with loved ones? You should be. The good things in your life, including your loved ones, come from God. He deserves the credit—and you deserve the glorious experience of giving it to Him.

MORE THOUGHTS FOR TODAY

As children observe an attitude and spirit of humility in us, our example will pave the way for them when they must admit to their Heavenly Father their own desperate need for guidance and forgiveness.

Annie Chapman

We are never stronger than the moment we admit we are weak.

Beth Moore

Although truth is not always humility, humility is always truth: the blunt acknowledgment that I owe my life, being, and salvation to Another. This fundamental act lies at the core of our response to grace.

Brennan Manning

God is against the proud, but he gives grace to the humble.

1 Peter 5:5 NCV

OUR PRAYER FOR TODAY

Heavenly Father, Jesus clothed Himself with humility when He chose to leave heaven and come to earth to live and die for us, His children. Jesus is our Master and our example. Clothe us with humility, Lord, so that we might be more like Your Son.

Amen

When Nobody
Is Watching

So I strive always to keep my conscience clear
before God and man.

Acts 24:16 NIV

It has been said that character is what we are when nobody is watching. How true. When we do things that we know aren't right, we try to hide them from our families and friends. But even then, God is watching.

Few things in life torment us more than a guilty conscience. And, few things in life provide more contentment than the knowledge that we are obeying the conscience that God has placed in our hearts.

If you sincerely want to create the best possible life for yourself and your loved ones, never forsake your conscience. And remember this: when you walk with God, your character will take care of itself...and you won't need to look over your shoulder to see who, besides God, is watching.

There is no pillow so soft as a clear conscience.

French Proverb

MORE THOUGHTS FOR TODAY

A quiet conscience sleeps in thunder.

Thomas Fuller

God desires the least degree of purity of conscience in you more than all the works you can perform.

St. John of the Cross

Let us come near to God with a sincere heart and a sure faith, because we have been made free from a guilty conscience, and our bodies have been washed with pure water.

Hebrews 10:22 NCV

OUR PRAYER FOR TODAY

Dear Lord, You speak to us through the gift of Your Holy Word. And, Father, You speak to us through that still small voice that tells us right from wrong.
Let us follow Your way, Lord. And show us Your plans so that we might serve You now and forever.
Amen

The Words We Speak

So then, rid yourselves of all evil, all lying, hypocrisy, jealousy,
and evil speech. As newborn babies want milk,
you should want the pure and simple teaching.
By it you can grow up and be saved.

1 Peter 2:1–2 NCV

All too often, we underestimate the importance of the words we speak. Whether we realize it or not, our words carry great weight and great power, especially when we are addressing our loved ones.

The Bible reminds us that "Reckless words pierce like a sword, but the tongue of the wise brings healing" (Proverbs 12:18 NIV). And Christ taught that "Out of the abundance of the heart the mouth speaks" (Matthew 12:34 NKJV).

Does the "abundance of your heart" produce a continuing flow of uplifting words for your loved one? And do you express those feelings many times each day? You should.

When you're angry, do you reign in your tongue? Proverbs 29:11 teaches, "A fool gives full vent to his anger, but a wise man keeps himself under control" (NIV).

So, if you'd like to build a better marriage—and if you'd like to keep building it day by day—think before you speak. Avoid angry outbursts. Refrain from constant criticism. Terminate tantrums. Negate negativism. Cease from being cynical. Instead, use Christ as your guide, and speak words of encouragement, hope, praise, and, above all, love—and speak them often.

MORE THOUGHTS FOR TODAY

Every word we speak, every action we take, has an effect on the totality of humanity. No one can escape that privilege—or that responsibility.

Laurie Beth Jones

The great test of a man's character is his tongue.

Oswald Chambers

Change the heart, and you change the speech.

Warren Wiersbe

Watch the way you talk. Let nothing foul or dirty come out of your mouth. Say only what helps, each word a gift.

Ephesians 4:29 MSG

OUR PRAYER FOR TODAY

Dear Lord, You have warned us that we will be judged by the words we speak. Keep us mindful that we have influence on many people, and let the words that we speak today be worthy of the One who has saved us forever.
Amen

Courtesy Matters

*Dear friend, when you extend hospitality to Christian brothers
and sisters, even when they are strangers,
you make the faith visible.*

3 John 1:5 MSG

Did Christ instruct us in matters of etiquette and courtesy? Of course He did. Christ's instructions are clear: "In everything, therefore, treat people the same way you want them to treat you, for this is the Law and the Prophets" (Matthew 7:12 NASB). Jesus did not say, "In some things, treat people as you wish to be treated." And, He did not say, "From time to time, treat others with kindness." Christ said that we should treat others as we wish to be treated in every aspect of our daily lives. This, of course, is a tall order indeed, but as Christians, we are commanded to do our best.

Today, be a little kinder than necessary to family members, friends, and total strangers. And, as you consider all the things that Christ has done in your life, honor Him with your words and with your deeds. He expects no less, and He deserves no less.

MORE THOUGHTS FOR TODAY

Only the courteous can love, but it is love that makes them courteous.

C. S. Lewis

Reach out and care for someone who needs the touch of hospitality. The time you spend caring today will be a love gift that will blossom into the fresh joy of God's Spirit in the future.

Emilie Barnes

You will accomplish more by kind words and a courteous manner than by anger and sharp rebuke, which should never be used, except in necessity.

St. Angela Merici

Out of respect for Christ, be courteously reverent to one another.
Ephesians 5:21 MSG

OUR PRAYER FOR TODAY

Help us, Lord, to treat everyone—especially each other—
with courtesy and respect. You have created each person
in Your own image; we are all Your children, Father.
So let us show kindness to all.
Amen

How to Start the Day

He awakens Me morning by morning,
He awakens My ear to hear as the learned.
The Lord God has opened My ear.

Isaiah 50:4-5 NKJV

How do you prepare for the day ahead? Do you awaken early enough to spend at least a few moments with God? Or do you sleep until the last possible minute, leaving no time to invest in matters of the heart and soul? Hopefully, you make a habit of spending precious moments each morning with your Creator. When you do, He will fill your heart, He will direct your thoughts, and He will guide your steps.

Your daily devotional time can be habit-forming, and should be. The first few minutes of each day are invaluable. Treat them that way, and offer them to God.

Maintenance of the devotional mood is indispensable to success in the Christian life.

A. W. Tozer

MORE THOUGHTS FOR TODAY

How motivating it has been for me to view my early morning devotions as time of retreat alone with Jesus, Who desires that I "come with Him by myself to a quiet place" in order to pray, read His Word, listen for His voice, and be renewed in my spirit.

Anne Graham Lotz

Meditating upon His Word will inevitably bring peace of mind, strength of purpose, and power for living.

Bill Bright

It is good to give thanks to the Lord, to sing praises to the Most High. It is good to proclaim your unfailing love in the morning, your faithfulness in the evening.

Psalm 92:1-2 NLT

OUR PRAYER FOR TODAY

Dear Lord, we come to You for guidance, for perspective, for wisdom, and for protection. Today and every day, we seek to obey Your Word and to honor Your Son.
Amen

Beyond the Doubts

If you don't know what you're doing, pray to the Father.
He loves to help. You'll get his help, and won't be condescended
to when you ask for it. Ask boldly, believingly, without
a second thought. People who "worry their prayers" are like
wind-whipped waves. Don't think you're going to get anything
from the Master that way, adrift at sea,
keeping all your options open.

James 1:5-8 MSG

Even the most faithful Christians are overcome by occasional bouts of fear and doubt. You are no different. When you feel that your faith is being tested to its limits, seek the comfort and assurance of the One who sent His Son as a sacrifice for you.

Have you ever felt your faith in God slipping away? If so, you are not alone. Every life—including yours—is a series of successes and failures, celebrations and disappointments, joys and sorrows, hopes and doubts.

But even when you feel very distant from God, remember that God is never distant from you. When you sincerely seek His presence, He will touch your heart, calm your fears, and restore your soul.

MORE THOUGHTS FOR TODAY

We basically have two choices to make in dealing with the mysteries of God. We can wrestle with Him or we can rest in Him.

Calvin Miller

Doubting may temporarily disturb, but will not permanently destroy, your faith in Christ

Charles Swindoll

Struggling with God over the issues of life doesn't show a lack of faith—that is faith.

Lee Strobel

Immediately the father of the child cried out and said with tears, "Lord, I believe; help my unbelief!"

Mark 9:24 NKJV

OUR PRAYER FOR TODAY

Dear Lord, when we are filled with uncertainty and doubt, give us faith. In the dark moments of life, keep us mindful of Your healing power and Your infinite love, so that we may live courageously and faithfully today and every day.
Amen

Your Duties to Him

*But as God has distributed to each one,
as the Lord has called each one, so let him walk.*

1 Corinthians 7:17 NKJV

Nobody needs to tell you the obvious: You have lots of responsibilities—obligations to yourself, to your family, to your community, and to your God. And which of these duties should take priority? The answer can be found in Matthew 6:33: "But seek first the kingdom of God and His righteousness, and all these things will be provided for you" (Holman CSB).

When you "seek first the kingdom of God," all your other obligations have a way of falling into place. When you obey God's Word and seek His will, your many responsibilities don't seem quite so burdensome. When you honor God with your time, your talents, and your prayers, you'll be much more likely to count your blessings instead of your troubles.

So do yourself and your loved ones a favor: take all your duties seriously, especially your duties to God. When you do, you'll discover that pleasing your Father in heaven isn't just the right thing to do; it's also the best way to live.

MORE THOUGHTS FOR TODAY

If you seek to know the path of your duty, use God as your compass.

C. H. Spurgeon

Discipleship usually brings us into the necessity of choice between duty and desire.

Elisabeth Elliot

The secret of a happy life is to do your duty and trust in God.

Sam Jones

So then each of us shall give account of himself to God.
Romans 14:12 NKJV

OUR PRAYER FOR TODAY

Dear Lord, today and every day, let us recognize our responsibilities, and let us fulfill them. And keep us mindful that absolutely no responsibility is greater than our obligation to follow in the footsteps of Your Son.
Amen

Ultimate Security

Finally, my brethren, be strong in the Lord and in the power of His might. Put on the whole armor of God, that you may be able to stand against the wiles of the devil.

Ephesians 6:10-11 NKJV

Make no mistake about it: God is your ultimate source of security. The world offers no safety nets, but God does. He sent His only begotten Son to offer you the priceless gift of eternal life. And now you are challenged to return God's love by obeying His commandments and honoring His Son.

When you and your spouse allow Christ to reign over your lives and your marriage, you will be secure. When you and your beloved feel God's presence and invite His Son to rule your hearts and your household, your family will be eternally blessed.

In a world filled with dangers and temptations, God is the ultimate armor. In a world filled with misleading messages, God's Word is the ultimate truth. In a world filled with more frustrations than we can count, God's Son offers the ultimate peace.

Will you and your spouse accept God's peace and wear God's armor against the dangers of our world? Hopefully so—because when you do, you can live courageously, knowing that you possess the ultimate security: God's unfailing love for you.

MORE THOUGHTS FOR TODAY

He goes before us, follows behind us, and hems us safe inside the realm of His protection.

Beth Moore

We can take great comfort that God never sleeps—so we can.

Dianna Booher

He is within and without. His Spirit dwells within me. His armor protects me. He goes before me and is behind me.

Mary Morrison Suggs

God is my shield, saving those whose hearts are true and right.
Psalm 7:10 NLT

OUR PRAYER FOR TODAY

Dear Lord, You have promised never to leave us or forsake us. You are always with us, protecting us and encouraging us. Whatever this day may bring, we thank You for Your love and for Your strength. We will lean upon You, Father, this day and forever.
Amen

Beyond Excuses

Let us live in a right way . . . clothe yourselves with
the Lord Jesus Christ and forget about
satisfying your sinful self.

Romans 13:13-14 NCV

Excuses are everywhere . . . excellence is not. Whether you're a stay-at-home mom or a corporate CEO, your work is a picture book of your priorities. So whatever your job description, it's up to you, and no one else, to become masterful at your craft. It's up to you to do your job right, and to do it right now.

Because we humans are such creative excuse-makers, all of the best excuses have already been taken—we've heard them all before.

So if you're wasting your time trying to concoct a new and improved excuse, don't bother. It's impossible. A far better strategy is this: do the work. Now. Then, let your excellent work speak loudly and convincingly for itself.

Replace your excuses with fresh determination.

Charles Swindoll

MORE THOUGHTS FOR TODAY

We need to stop focusing on our lacks and stop giving out excuses and start looking at and listening to Jesus.

Anne Graham Lotz

Never use your problem as an excuse for bad attitudes or behavior.

Joyce Meyer

You, therefore, have no excuse, you who pass judgment on someone else, for at whatever point you judge the other, you are condemning yourself.

Romans 2:1 NIV

OUR PRAYER FOR TODAY

Heavenly Father, how easy it is to make excuses.
But, we understand the need to accomplish important
work—work for our family and work for You. Help us,
Father, to strive for excellence, not excuses.
Amen

Listening to God

The one who is from God listens to God's words.
This is why you don't listen, because you are not from God.

John 8:47 Holman CSB

Sometimes God speaks loudly and clearly. More often, He speaks in a quiet voice—and if you are wise, you will be listening carefully when He does. To do so, you must carve out quiet moments each day to study His Word and sense His direction.

Can you quiet yourself long enough to listen to your conscience? Are you attuned to the subtle guidance of your intuition? Are you willing to pray sincerely and then to wait quietly for God's response? Hopefully so. Usually God refrains from sending His messages on stone tablets or city billboards. More often, He communicates in subtler ways. If you sincerely desire to hear His voice, you must listen carefully, and you must do so in the silent corners of your quiet, willing heart.

When we come to Jesus stripped of pretensions, with a needy spirit, ready to listen, He meets us at the point of need.

Catherine Marshall

MORE THOUGHTS FOR TODAY

An essential condition of listening to God is that the mind should not be distracted by thoughts of resentment, ill-temper, hatred or vengeance, all of which are comprised in the general term, the wrath of man.

R. V. G. Tasker

In prayer, the ear is of first importance. It is of equal importance with the tongue, but the ear must be named first. We must listen to God.

S. D. Gordon

Listen in silence before me....

Isaiah 41:1 NLT

OUR PRAYER FOR TODAY

Lord, help us listen carefully to each other,
to our family members, to our friends,
and—most importantly—to You.
Amen

Learning His Lessons

*A wise person pays attention to correction
that will improve his life.*

Proverbs 15:31 ICB

One way that we learn about God is by learning the lessons that He is trying so desperately to teach us. But when it comes to learning God's lessons, most of us can be quite hardheaded. Why? Because we are, by nature, stubborn creatures; and because we seem destined, at times, to make things hard on ourselves.

As we go about the business of learning life's lessons, we can either do things the easy way or the hard way. The easy way can be summed up as follows: when God tries to teach us something, we learn it . . . the first time! Unfortunately, too many of us learn much more slowly than that.

When we resist God's instruction, He continues to teach, whether we like it or not. Our challenge, then, is to discern God's lessons from the experiences of everyday life. Hopefully, we learn those lessons sooner rather than later because the sooner we do so, the sooner He can move on to the next lesson and the next, and the next . . .

MORE THOUGHTS FOR TODAY

The wonderful thing about God's schoolroom is that we get to grade our own papers. You see, He doesn't test us so He can learn how well we're doing. He tests us so we can discover how well we're doing.

Charles Swindoll

The wise man gives proper appreciation in his life to this past. He learns to sift the sawdust of heritage in order to find the nuggets that make the current moment have any meaning.

Grady Nutt

I hope you don't mind me telling you all this? One can learn only by seeing one's mistakes.

C. S. Lewis

It is not good to have zeal without knowledge, nor to be hasty and miss the way.

Proverbs 19:2 NIV

OUR PRAYER FOR TODAY

Dear Lord, we have so much to learn. Help us to watch, to listen, to think, and to learn, every day of our lives.
Amen

Beyond Failure

If we confess our sins to him, he is faithful and just
to forgive us and to cleanse us from every wrong.

1 John 1:9 NLT

The occasional disappointments and failures of life are inevitable. Such setbacks are simply the price that we must occasionally pay for our willingness to take risks as we follow our dreams. But even when we encounter bitter disappointments, we must never lose faith.

The reassuring words of Hebrews 10:36 remind us that when we persevere, we will eventually receive that which God has promised. What's required is perseverance, not perfection.

When we encounter the inevitable difficulties of life here on earth, God stands ready to protect us. Our responsibility, of course, is to ask Him for protection. When we call upon Him in heartfelt prayer, He will answer—in His own time and according to His own plan—and He will heal us. And, while we are waiting for God's plans to unfold and for His healing touch to restore us, we can be comforted in the knowledge that our Creator can overcome any obstacle, even if we cannot.

MORE THOUGHTS FOR TODAY

One of the ways God refills us after failure is through the blessing of Christian fellowship. Just experiencing the joy of simple activities shared with other children of God can have a healing effect on us.

Anne Graham Lotz

The almighty Father will use life's reverses to move you forward.

Barbara Johnson

Never imagine that you can be a loser by trusting in God.

C. H. Spurgeon

If you hide your sins, you will not succeed. If you confess and reject them, you will receive mercy.

Proverbs 28:13 NCV

OUR PRAYER FOR TODAY

Dear Lord, when we encounter failures and
disappointments, keep us mindful that You are in control.
Let us persevere—even if our souls are troubled—
and let us follow Your Son,
Jesus Christ, this day and forever.
Amen

Too Busy?

Don't burn out; keep yourselves fueled and aflame.
Be alert servants of the Master, cheerfully expectant.
Don't quit in hard times; pray all the harder.

Romans 12:11-12 MSG

Are you making time each day to praise God and to study His Word? If so, you know firsthand the blessings that He offers those who worship Him consistently and sincerely. But, if you have unintentionally allowed the hustle and bustle of your busy day to come between you and your Creator, then you must slow down, take a deep breath, and rearrange your priorities.

God loved this world so much that He sent His Son to save it. And now only one real question remains for you: what will you do in response to God's love? The answer should be obvious: God must come first in your life. He is the giver of all good things, and He is the One who sent His Son so that you might have eternal life. He deserves your prayers, your obedience, your stewardship, and your love—and He deserves these things all day every day, not just on Sunday mornings.

MORE THOUGHTS FOR TODAY

The busier we are, the easier it is to worry, the greater the temptation to worry, the greater the need to be alone with God.

Charles Stanley

Noise and words and frenzied, hectic schedules dull our senses, closing our ears to His still, small voice and making us numb to His touch.

Charles Swindoll

Careful planning puts you ahead in the long run; hurry and scurry puts you further behind.

Proverbs 21:5 MSG

OUR PRAYER FOR TODAY

Dear Lord, when the quickening pace of life leaves us with little time for worship or for praise, help us reorder our priorities. When the demands of the day leave us distracted and discouraged, let us turn to Jesus for the peace that only He can give. And then, when we have accepted the spiritual abundance that can be ours through Christ, let us share His message and His love.

Amen

Celebrating Today

This is the day which the LORD has made;
let us rejoice and be glad in it.

Psalm 118:24 NASB

The 118th Psalm reminds us that today, like every other day, is a cause for celebration. God gives us this day; He fills it to the brim with possibilities, and He challenges us to use it for His purposes. The day is presented to us fresh and clean at midnight, free of charge, but we must beware: Today is a non-renewable resource—once it's gone, it's gone forever. Our responsibility, of course, is to use this day in the service of God's will and according to His commandments.

Today, treasure the time that God has given you. Give Him the glory and the praise and the thanksgiving that He deserves. And search for the hidden possibilities that God has placed along your path. This day is a priceless gift from God, so use it joyfully and encourage others to do likewise. After all, this is the day the Lord has made....

The church is the last place on earth to be solemn . . . provided you have lived right.

Sam Jones

MORE THOUGHTS FOR TODAY

Not every day of our lives is overflowing with joy and celebration. But there are moments when our hearts nearly burst within us for the sheer joy of being alive. The first sight of our newborn babies, the warmth of love in another's eyes, the fresh scent of rain on a hot summer's eve—moments like these renew in us a heartfelt appreciation for life.

Gwen Ellis

Some of us seem so anxious about avoiding hell that we forget to celebrate our journey toward heaven.

Philip Yancey

A happy heart is like a continual feast.

Proverbs 15:15 NCV

OUR PRAYER FOR TODAY

Dear Lord, help us remember that every day is cause
for celebration. Today we will try our best to keep
joy in our hearts. We will celebrate the life
You have given us here on earth and the eternal life
that will be ours in heaven.
Amen

Financial Common Sense

For I am the Lord, I do not change. Will a man rob God?
Yet you have robbed Me! But you say, in what way have
we robbed You? In tithes and offerings. You are cursed
with a curse, for you have robbed Me, even this whole nation.
Bring all the tithes into the storehouse,
that there may be food in My house.

Malachi 3:6,8-10 NKJV

Sometimes, our financial struggles are simply manifestations of the inner conflict that we feel when we stray from God's path. The beautiful words of John 14:27 remind us that Jesus offers us peace, not as the world gives, but as He alone gives. Our challenge is to accept Christ's peace into our hearts and then, as best we can, to share His peace with our families and friends.

When we summon the courage and the determination to implement a sensible financial plan, we invite peace into our lives. But, we should never confuse earthly peace (with a small "p") with spiritual Peace (the heavenly Peace—with a capital "P"—that flows from the Prince of Peace).

When we accept Jesus as our personal Savior, we are transformed by His grace. We are then free to accept the spiritual abundance and peace that can be ours through the power of the risen Christ.

Have you found the genuine peace that can be yours through Christ? Or are you still rushing after the illusion of "peace and happiness" that the world promises but cannot deliver? Today, as a gift to yourself and to your loved ones, claim the inner peace that is your spiritual birthright: the peace of Jesus Christ. It is offered freely; it has been paid for in full; it is yours for the asking. So ask. And then share.

Financial peace can, and should, be yours. But the spiritual peace that stems from your personal relationship with Jesus must be yours if you are to receive the eternal abundance of our Lord. Claim that abundance today.

MORE THOUGHTS FOR TODAY

If your outgo exceeds your income, then your upkeep will be your downfall.

John Maxwell

And my God shall supply all your need according to His riches in glory by Christ Jesus.

Philippians 4:19 NKJV

OUR PRAYER FOR TODAY

Lord, there are many things we desire, and many things
we may never have. But we can have peace.
We will trust You to care for our needs, Father,
today, tomorrow, and forever.
Amen

Fitness Matters

Whatever you eat or drink or whatever you do,
you must do all for the glory of God.

1 Corinthians 10:31 NLT

Are you shaping up or spreading out? Do you eat sensibly and exercise regularly, or do you spend most of your time on the couch with a Twinkie in one hand and a clicker in the other? Are you choosing to treat your body like a temple or a trash heap? How you answer these questions will help determine how long you live and how well you live.

Physical fitness is a choice, a choice that requires discipline—it's as simple as that. So, do yourself this favor: treat your body like a one-of-a-kind gift from God . . . because that's precisely what your body is.

You can look at your calorie count in the same way you might look at a bank account. Every mouthful of food is a deposit and every activity that requires energy is a withdrawal. If we deposit more then we withdraw our surplus grows larger and larger.

Jim Maxwell

MORE THOUGHTS FOR TODAY

Our primary motivation should not be for more energy or to avoid a heart attack but to please God with our bodies.

Carole Lewis

Whenever I read the words of Isaiah that say those who "wait on the Lord" shall "run and not be weary" and "walk and not faint," I'm reminded of how naturally spiritual development and endurance exercise go together.

Dr. Kenneth Cooper

Didn't you realize that your body is a sacred place, the place of the Holy Spirit? Don't you see that you can't live however you please, squandering what God paid such a high price for? The physical part of you is not some piece of property belonging to the spiritual part of you.

1 Corinthians 6:19 MSG

OUR PRAYER FOR TODAY

Lord, all that we are belongs to you. As we serve You
with all that we are and all that we have,
help us honor You by caring for the bodies
that You have given us.
Amen

What's Your Focus?

Let us lay aside every weight and the sin that so easily ensnares us, and run with endurance the race that lies before us, keeping our eyes on Jesus, the source and perfecter of our faith.

Hebrews 12:1-2 Holman CSB

What is your focus today? Are you willing to focus your thoughts and energies on God's blessings and upon His will for your life? Or will you turn your thoughts to other things? Before you answer that question, consider this: God created you in His own image, and He wants you to experience joy and abundance. But, God will not force His joy upon you; you must claim it for yourself.

This day—and every day hereafter—is a chance to celebrate the life that God has given you. It's also a chance to give thanks to the One who has offered you more blessings than you can possibly count.

Today, why not focus your thoughts on the joy that is rightfully yours in Christ? Why not take time to celebrate God's glorious creation? Why not trust your hopes instead of your fears? When you do, you will think optimistically about yourself and your world . . . and you can then share your optimism with others. They'll be better for it, and so will you. But not necessarily in that order.

MORE THOUGHTS FOR TODAY

One can get just as much exultation in losing oneself in a little thing as in a big thing. It is nice to think how one can be recklessly lost in a daisy!

Anne Morrow Lindbergh

Just like commercial organizations need to get their focus off themselves, we as individual Christians and collective churches need to recalibrate our sights on the target God has given us: spiritually lost people.

Bill Hybels

Give your entire attention to what God is doing right now, and don't get worked up about what may or may not happen tomorrow. God will help you deal with whatever hard things come up when the time comes.

Matthew 6:34 MSG

OUR PRAYER FOR TODAY

Dear Lord, help us face this day with optimism and hope.
And let us focus our thoughts on You
and Your incomparable gifts.
Amen

Walk With Him

Then he told them what they could expect for themselves:
"Anyone who intends to come with me has to let me lead."

Luke 9:23 MSG

Jesus walks with you. Are you walking with Him? Hopefully, you will choose to walk with Him today and every day of your life.

Jesus loved you so much that He endured unspeakable humiliation and suffering for you. How will you respond to Christ's sacrifice? Will you take up His cross and follow Him (Luke 9:23) or will you choose another path? When you place your hopes squarely at the foot of the cross, when you place Jesus squarely at the center of your life, you will be blessed. If you seek to be a worthy disciple of Jesus, you must acknowledge that He never comes "next." He is always first.

Do you hope to fulfill God's purpose for your life? Do you seek a life of abundance and peace? Do you intend to be Christian, not just in name, but in deed? Then follow Christ. Follow Him by picking up His cross today and every day that you live. When you do, you will quickly discover that Christ's love has the power to change everything, including you.

MORE THOUGHTS FOR TODAY

A disciple is a follower of Christ. That means you take on His priorities as your own. His agenda becomes your agenda. His mission becomes your mission.

Charles Stanley

Think of this—we may live together with Him here and now, a daily walking with Him who loved us and gave Himself for us.

Elisabeth Elliot

Christ tells us that if we want to join Him, we will travel the way He took. Surely it is not right that the Son of God should go His way on the path of shame while the sons of men walk the way of worldly honor.

John of Avila

Then he told them what they could expect for themselves: "Anyone who intends to come with me has to let me lead."

Luke 9:23 MSG

OUR PRAYER FOR TODAY

Dear Lord, You sent Your Son so that we might have abundant life and eternal life. Thank You, Father, for our Savior, Christ Jesus. We will follow Him, honor Him, and obey His teachings, this day and every day.

Amen

Priorities

First pay attention to me, and then relax.
Now you can take it easy—you're in good hands.

Proverbs 1:33 MSG

It takes time to build a strong marriage . . . lots of time. Yet we live in a world where time seems to be an ever-shrinking commodity as we rush from place to place with seldom a moment to spare.

Has the busy pace of life robbed you of sufficient time with your loved ones? If so, it's time to adjust your priorities. And God can help.

When you fervently ask God to help you prioritize your life, He will give you guidance. When you seek His guidance every day, your Creator will reveal Himself in a variety of ways. As a follower of Christ, you must do no less.

When you allow God to help you organize your day, you'll soon discover that there is ample time for your spouse and your family. When you make God a full partner in every aspect of your life, He will lead you along the proper path: His path. When you allow God to reign over your heart, He will honor you with spiritual blessings that are simply too numerous to count. So, as you plan for the day ahead, make God's priorities your priorities. When you do, every other priority will have a tendency to fall neatly into place.

MORE THOUGHTS FOR TODAY

Oh, that we might discern the will of God, surrender to His calling, resign the masses of activities, and do a few things well. What a legacy that would be for our children.

Beth Moore

The moment you wake up each morning, all your wishes and hopes for the day rush at you like wild animals. And the first job each morning consists in shoving it all back; in listening to that other voice, taking that other point of view, letting that other, larger, stronger, quieter life coming flowing in.

C. S. Lewis

And I pray this: that your love will keep on growing in knowledge and every kind of discernment, so that you can determine what really matters and can be pure and blameless in the day of Christ.
Philippians 1:9 Holman CSB

OUR PRAYER FOR TODAY

Dear Lord, let Your priorities be our priorities.
Let Your will be our will. Let Your Word be our guide,
and let us grow in faith and in wisdom
this day and every day.
Amen

Generosity Now

God has given gifts to each of you from his great variety
of spiritual gifts. Manage them well so that God's generosity
can flow through you.

1 Peter 4:10 NLT

ymn writer Fanny Crosby wrote, "To God be the glory; great thing He hath done! So loved He the world that He gave us His son." God's love for us is so complete that He sent Jesus to this earth so that we, His believers, might have eternal life: "But God demonstrates his own love for us in this: While we were still sinners, Christ died for us" (Romans 5:8 NIV).

We, as Christ's followers, are challenged to share His love. We do so, in part, by dealing generously and lovingly with others.

When we walk each day with Christ—and obey the commandments found in God's Holy Word—we are worthy ambassadors for Him. Just as Christ has been—and will always be—the ultimate friend to His flock, so should we be Christlike in our love and generosity to those in pain and to those in need. When we share the love of Christ, we share a priceless gift; may we share it today and every day that we live.

MORE THOUGHTS FOR TODAY

Giving from a grateful heart and expecting nothing in return is a sweet offering to the One who owns everything I have anyway. It's the very least I can do. And as I give, I experience God's grace.

Mary Hunt

To show great love for God and our neighbor, we need not do great things. It is how much love we put in the doing that makes our offering something beautiful for God.

Mother Teresa

Let us give according to our incomes, lest God make our incomes match our gifts.

Peter Marshall

Now this I say, he who sows sparingly will also reap sparingly, and he who sows bountifully will also reap bountifully. Each one must do just as he has purposed in his heart, not grudgingly or under compulsion, for God loves a cheerful giver.

2 Corinthians 9:6-7 NASB

OUR PRAYER FOR TODAY

Dear Lord, You have been so generous with us; let us be generous with others. Help us to focus on the needs of others. And, make us humble givers, Lord, so that all the glory and the praise might be Yours.

Amen

God Can Handle It

Can you understand the secrets of God? His limits are higher
than the heavens; you cannot reach them!
They are deeper than the grave; you cannot understand them!
His limits are longer than the earth and wider than the sea.

Job 11:7-9 NCV

It's a promise that is made over and over again in the Bible: Whatever "it" is, God can handle it.

Life isn't always easy. Far from it! Sometimes, life can be very, very tough. But even then, even during our darkest moments, we're protected by a loving Heavenly Father. When we're worried, God can reassure us; when we're sad, God can comfort us. When our hearts are broken, God is not just near; He is here. So we must lift our thoughts and prayers to Him. When we do, He will answer our prayers. Why? Because He is our shepherd, and He has promised to protect us now and forever.

Sovereignty means that God alone ultimately has the right to declare what creation should be.

Stanley Grenz

MORE THOUGHTS FOR TODAY

When considering the size of your problems, there are two categories that you should never worry about: the problems that are small enough for you to handle, and the ones that aren't too big for God to handle.

Marie T. Freeman

Don't think so much about who is for or against you, rather give all your care that God be with you in everything you do.

Thomas à Kempis

For now we see indistinctly, as in a mirror, but then face to face. Now I know in part, but then I will know fully, as I am fully known.

1 Corinthians 13:12 Holman CSB

OUR PRAYER FOR TODAY

Dear Lord, You rule over our world—and we will allow You to rule over our hearts. We will obey Your commandments, we will study Your Word, and we will trust You to protect us today, tomorrow, and forever.
Amen

Be Still

Be still before the Lord and wait patiently for Him.

Psalm 37:7 NIV

Ours is a fast-paced world. The demands of the day can seem overwhelming at times, but when we slow ourselves down and seek the presence of a loving God, we invite His peace into our hearts.

Do you carve out quiet moments each day to offer thanksgiving and praise to your Creator? You should. During these moments of stillness, you will often sense the infinite love and power of our Lord.

The familiar words of Psalm 46:10 remind us to "Be still, and know that I am God." When we do so, we encounter the awesome presence of our loving Heavenly Father, and we are blessed beyond words.

Be still, and in the quiet moments, listen to the voice of your Heavenly Father. His words can renew your spirit—no one knows you and your needs like He does.

Janet L. Weaver Smith

MORE THOUGHTS FOR TODAY

So wait before the Lord. Wait in the stillness. And in that stillness, assurance will come to you. You will know that you are heard; you will know that your Lord ponders the voice of your humble desires; you will hear quiet words spoken to you yourself, perhaps to your grateful surprise and refreshment.

Amy Carmichael

Let your loneliness be transformed into a holy aloneness. Sit still before the Lord. Remember Naomi's word to Ruth: "Sit still, my daughter, until you see how the matter will fall."

Elisabeth Elliot

Be still, and know that I am God....

Psalm 46:10 KJV

OUR PRAYER FOR TODAY

Dear Lord, let us be still before You. When we are hurried or distracted, slow us down and redirect our thoughts. When we are confused, give us perspective. Keep us mindful, Father, that You are always with us. And let us sense Your presence now and forever.

Amen

Saved by Grace

But God, who is abundant in mercy, because of His great love
that He had for us, made us alive with the Messiah even though
we were dead in trespasses. By grace you are saved!

Ephesians 2:4-5 Holman CSB

We are saved, not by our own righteousness, but by God's grace. God's priceless gift of eternal life is not a reward for our good deeds; it is a manifestation of God's infinite love for those who worship Him and accept His Son as their Savior.

Are you absolutely certain that you have accepted the gift of salvation? If not, drop to your knees this very instant and accept Christ as your personal Savior. And, if you are already the thankful recipient of eternal life through Christ Jesus, use this day as an opportunity to share your testimony with friends and family members.

Jesus is the sovereign friend and ultimate Savior of mankind. Christ showed enduring love for us by willingly sacrificing His own life so that we might have eternal life. Let us love Him, praise Him, and share His message of salvation with our neighbors and with the world.

MORE THOUGHTS FOR TODAY

The grace of God is infinite and eternal. As it had no beginning, so it can have no end, and being an attribute of God, it is as boundless as infinitude.

A. W. Tozer

Jesus has affected human society like no other. The incomparable Christ is the good news. And what makes it such good news is that man is so undeserving but that God is so gracious.

John MacArthur

My grace is sufficient for you, for My strength is made perfect in weakness.

2 Corinthians 12:9 NKJV

OUR PRAYER FOR TODAY

Lord, Your grace is a gift that cannot be earned. It is a gift that was given freely when we accepted Your Son as our personal Savior. Freely have we received Your gifts, Father. Let us freely share our gifts, our possessions, our time, our energy, and our faith. And let us bring honor to You and to Your Son, now and forever.

Amen

Accepting His Love

We know how much God loves us, and we have put our trust in him. God is love, and all who live in love live in God, and God lives in them.

1 John 4:16 NLT

Make no mistake about it: God loves our world. He loves it so much, in fact, that He sent His only begotten Son to die for our sins. And now we, as believers, are challenged to return God's love by obeying His commandments and honoring His Son.

When you and your spouse allow Christ to reign over your lives and your marriage, you will be transformed: you will feel differently about yourselves, your marriage, your family, and your world. When you and your beloved feel God's presence and invite His Son to rule your hearts and your household, your family will be eternally blessed.

God loved this world so much that He sent His Son to save it. And now only one real question remains: what will you and yours do in response to God's love? The answer should be obvious: If you haven't already done so, accept Jesus Christ as Your Savior. He's waiting patiently for you, but please don't make Him wait another minute longer.

MORE THOUGHTS FOR TODAY

If God had a refrigerator, your picture would be on it. If He had a wallet, your photo would be in it. He sends you flowers every spring and a sunrise every morning.

Max Lucado

Love has its source in God, for love is the very essence of His being.

Kay Arthur

Joy comes from knowing God loves me and knows who I am and where I'm going . . . that my future is secure as I rest in Him.

Jame Dobson

As the Father loved Me, I also have loved you; abide in My love.

John 15:9 NKJV

OUR PRAYER FOR TODAY

Thank You, Lord, for Your love. Your love is boundless, infinite, and eternal. Today, we will pause and reflect upon Your love for us, and we will share that love with the people who cross our paths. And, as an expression of our love for You, Father, we will share the saving message of Your Son with a world in desperate need of His peace.

Amen

DAY 71

Total Commitment

So let's keep focused on that goal [reaching out to Christ],
those of us who want everything God has for us. If any of you
have something else in mind, something less than
total commitment, God will clear your blurred vision,
you'll see it yet!

Philippians 3:15, 16 MSG

Sometimes, it's easy to be in love—just ask any blissful young couple who recently got engaged! But sometimes, love isn't quite as easy as that—just ask any long-married couple who faces health problems, financial difficulties, family tragedy, or any other significant brand of trouble. Honest-to-goodness love is strong enough to weather these storms because honest-to-goodness love isn't a feeling that comes and goes; it's a level of commitment that remains steady and strong, even when times are tough.

Every marriage, like every life, will encounter days of hardship and pain. It is during these difficult days that husbands and wives discover precisely what their marriage is made of.

God's Word makes it clear: genuine love is committed love. Genuine love is more than a feeling . . . it is a decision to make love endure, no matter what. So, if you want your love to last forever, then you and your spouse must be totally committed to each other. When you are, then you can rest assured that the two of you—plus God—can handle anything that comes your way.

MORE THOUGHTS FOR TODAY

Wherever your marriage is today, make or reaffirm your unyielding commitment to its permanence.

Ed Young

So I go to church, not because of any legalistic or moralistic reasons, but because I am a hungry sheep who needs to be fed; and for the same reason that I wear a wedding ring: a public witness of a private commitment.

Madeleine L'Engle

Any time you make a commitment to something, it will be tested.

John Maxwell

A man leaves his father and mother and bonds with his wife, and they become one flesh.

Genesis 2:24 Holman CSB

OUR PRAYER FOR TODAY

Dear Lord, give us the strength and the wisdom to
be totally committed to You. Guide us away from the
temptations and distractions of this world, so that we
might honor You with our thoughts,
our actions, and our prayers.
Amen

Arguments Lost

A hot-tempered man stirs up dissention,
but a patient man calms a quarrel.

Proverbs 15:18 NIV

Arguments are seldom won but often lost. When we engage in petty squabbles, our losses usually outpace our gains. When we acquire the unfortunate habit of habitual bickering, we do harm to our spouses, to our friends, to our families, to our coworkers, and to ourselves.

Time and again, God's Word warns us that most arguments are a monumental waste of time, of energy, of life. In Titus, we are warned to refrain from "foolish arguments," and with good reason. Such arguments usually do more for the devil than they do for God.

So the next time you're tempted to engage in a silly squabble, whether inside the church or outside it, refrain. When you do, you'll put a smile on God's face, and you'll send the devil packing.

The Gospel has to be experienced, not argued!

Grady Nutt

MORE THOUGHTS FOR TODAY

Some fights are lost even though we win. A bulldog can whip a skunk, but it just isn't worth it.

Vance Havner

Whatever you do when conflicts arise, be wise. Fight against jumping to quick conclusions and seeing only your side. There are always two sides on the streets of conflict. Look both ways.

Charles Swindoll

But I tell you that men will have to give account on the day of judgment for every careless word they have spoken. For by your words you will be acquitted, and by your words you will be condemned.

Matthew 12:36-37 NIV

OUR PRAYER FOR TODAY

Dear Lord, when we are tempted to be argumentative,
keep us calm. When we fall prey to pettiness, restore our
sense of perspective. When we are gripped by irrational
anger, give us serenity. Let us show our thankfulness
to You by offering forgiveness to others.
And, when we do, may others see Your love
reflected in our words and our deeds.
Amen

Strengthening Your Faith and Your Marriage

Be on the alert, stand firm in the faith, act like men, be strong.
1 Corinthians 16:13 NASB

Would you and your spouse like to strengthen the bonds of your marriage? Here's a wonderful place to start: by strengthening your faith in God.

Every life and every marriage is a series of successes and failures, celebrations and disappointments, joys and sorrows. Every step of the way, through every triumph and tragedy, God will stand by your side and strengthen you . . . if you have faith in Him. Jesus taught His disciples that if they had faith, they could move mountains. You can too.

When a suffering woman sought healing by merely touching the hem of His cloak, Jesus replied, "Daughter, be of good comfort; thy faith hath made thee whole" (Matthew 9:22 KJV). The message to believers of every generation is clear: we must live by faith today and every day.

When you and your spouse place your faith, your trust, indeed your life in the hands of Christ Jesus, you'll be amazed at the marvelous things He can do with you and through you. So strengthen your faith and you marriage through praise, through worship, through Bible study, and through prayer. And trust God's plans. With Him, all things are possible, and He stands ready to open a world of possibilities to you and yours . . . if you have faith.

MORE THOUGHTS FOR TODAY

Forgive us our lack of faith, lest ulcers become our badge of disbelief.

Peter Marshall

I want my life to be a faith-filled leap into His arms, knowing He will be there—not that everything will go as I want, but that He will be there and that this will be enough.

Sheila Walsh

For whatever is born of God overcomes the world. And this is the victory that has overcome the world—our faith.

1 John 5:4 NKJV

OUR PRAYER FOR TODAY

Dear Lord, keep us mindful that You are always near
and that You can overcome any challenge. With Your love
and Your power, Father, we can live courageously
and faithfully today and every day.
Amen

Sharing Your Testimony

But the following night the Lord stood by him and said,
"Be of good cheer, Paul; for as you have testified for Me."

Acts 23:11 NKJV

Have you and your spouse made the decision to allow Christ to reign over your hearts? If so, you both have important stories to tell.

In his second letter to Timothy, Paul shares a message to believers of every generation when he writes, "God has not given us a spirit of timidity" (1:7). Paul's meaning is clear: When sharing our testimonies, we, as Christians, must be courageous, forthright, and unashamed. But sometimes, because we are fearful that we might be rebuffed, we may be slow to acknowledge the changes that Christ has made in our lives. Nonetheless, we must rise above our fears in order to share the story of Jesus with a world that desperately needs to hear His story.

When we let other people know the details of our faith, we assume an important responsibility: the responsibility of making certain that our actions give credence to our words. Once we have shared our testimonies, we must also be willing to serve as shining examples of righteousness—undeniable examples of the changes that Jesus makes in the lives of those who accept Him as their Savior.

Are you willing to follow in the footsteps of Jesus? If so, you must also be willing to talk about Him. And make no mistake: the time to express your belief in Him is now. You know how He has touched your own heart; help Him do the same for others.

MORE THOUGHTS FOR TODAY

When people share their experience of transformation, crediting the living, loving God with their visible, tangible change, this validates faith and allows others to hope, search, and find that God is powerful, present, and personal in our time.

Becky Tirabassi

The sermon of your life in tough times ministers to people more powerfully than the most eloquent speaker.

Bill Bright

But respect Christ as the holy Lord in your hearts. Always be ready to answer everyone who asks you to explain about the hope you have.

1 Peter 3:15 NCV

OUR PRAYER FOR TODAY

Dear Lord, let us share the Good News of Your Son Jesus; let the lives that we live and the words that we speak bear testimony to our faith in Him. Help us share our faith with others so that they, too, might dedicate their lives to Christ and receive His eternal gifts.

Amen

Changes

*John said, "Change your hearts and lives because
the kingdom of heaven is near."*

Matthew 3:2 NCV

The world is in a state of constant change, and so is your family. Kids are growing up and moving out; loved ones are growing older and passing on. Everything around you may seem to be in a state of flux, but you can be comforted: although the world is in a state of constant change, God is not.

If your children seem to be growing up before your eyes, don't panic. And even if other changes in your life are unfolding at a furious pace, your Heavenly Father is the rock that cannot be shaken. His Word promises, "I am the Lord, I do not change" (Malachi 3:6 NKJV).

Remember that "Jesus Christ is the same yesterday, today, and forever" (Hebrews 13:8 NKJV). And rest assured: It is precisely because your Savior does not change that you and your family can face the transitions of life with courage for today and hope for tomorrow.

The secret of contentment in the midst of change is found in having roots in the changeless Christ—the same yesterday, today and forever.

Ed Young

MORE THOUGHTS FOR TODAY

Conditions are always changing; therefore, I must not be dependent upon conditions. What matters supremely is my soul and my relationship to God.

Corrie ten Boom

We are either the masters or the victims of our attitudes. It is a matter of personal choice. Who we are today is the result of choices we made yesterday. Tomorrow, we will become what we choose today. To change means to choose to change.

John Maxwell

There is a time for everything, and a season for every activity under heaven.

Ecclesiastes 3:1 NIV

OUR PRAYER FOR TODAY

Dear Lord, our family changes, but You are unchanging.
When we face the inevitable transitions of life,
we will turn to You for strength and assurance.
Let our trust in You—like Your love for us—
be unchanging and everlasting.
Amen

The Right Kind of Fear

Honor all people. Love the brotherhood.
Fear God. Honor the king.

1 Peter 2:17 NKJV

D o you have a healthy, fearful respect for God's power? If so, you are both wise and obedient. And, because you are a thoughtful believer, you also understand that genuine wisdom begins with a profound appreciation for God's limitless power.

God praises humility and punishes pride. That's why God's greatest servants will always be those humble men and women who care less for their own glory and more for God's glory. In God's kingdom, the only way to achieve greatness is to shun it. And the only way to be wise is to understand these facts: God is great; He is all-knowing; and He is all-powerful. We must respect Him, and we must humbly obey His commandments, or we must accept the consequences of our misplaced pride.

The remarkable thing about fearing God is that when you fear God, you fear nothing else, whereas if you do not fear God, you fear everything else.

Oswald Chambers

MORE THOUGHTS FOR TODAY

If we do not tremble before God, the world's system seems wonderful to us and pleasantly consumes us.

James Montgomery Boice

A healthy fear of God will do much to deter us from sin.

Charles Swindoll

The fear of God is the death of every other fear.

C. H. Spurgeon

Fear the LORD your God, serve him only and take your oaths in his name.

Deuteronomy 6:13 NIV

OUR PRAYER FOR TODAY

Lord, You love us and protect us. We praise You,
Father, for Your grace, and we respect You
for Your infinite power. Let our greatest fear in life
be the fear of displeasing You.
Amen

The Art of Cooperation

And if a kingdom be divided against itself, that kingdom cannot stand. And if a house be divided against itself, that house cannot stand.

Mark 3:24-25 KJV

Have you and your mate learned the art of cooperation? If so, you have learned the wisdom of "give and take," not the foolishness of "me first." Cooperation is the art of compromising on many little things while keeping your eye on one big thing: your relationship.

Cooperative relationships flourish over time. But, whenever couples fail to cooperate with each other, they sow the seeds of dissatisfaction, frustration, and competition within their marriage. In such cases, marriage partners may find themselves engaged in an unwitting "contest" to receive their "fair share" from the relationship. These types of struggles inevitably create far more problems than they solve.

If you're like most of us, you're probably a little bit headstrong: you probably want most things done in a fashion resembling the popular song "My Way." But, if you are observant, you will notice that those people who always insist upon "my way or the highway" usually end up with "the highway."

A better strategy for all concerned (including you) is to abandon the search for "my way" and search instead for "our way." The best marriages are those in which both partners learn how to "give and take" . . . with both partners trying to give a little more than they take.

MORE THOUGHTS FOR TODAY

Cooperation is a two-way street, but for too many couples, it's the road less traveled.

Marie T. Freeman

Weak things united become strong.

Thomas Fuller

You're blessed when you can show people how to cooperate instead of compete or fight. That's when you discover who you really are, and your place in God's family.

Matthew 5:9 MSG

OUR PRAYER FOR TODAY

Lord, so much more can be accomplished when we join
together to fulfill our common goals and desires.
As we seek to fulfill Your will for our lives, let us also
join with others to accomplish Your greater good
for our families, for our communities,
for our nation and for our world.
Amen

Thank Him

In everything give thanks; for this is the will of God
in Christ Jesus for you.

1 Thessalonians 5:18 NKJV

Your life and your marriage are gifts from God: celebrate them and give thanks. When you celebrate the gifts of life and love, your thankful heart will serve as a powerful blessing to your loved ones.

Every good gift comes from God. As believers who have been saved by a risen Christ, we owe unending thanksgiving to our Heavenly Father. Yet sometimes, amid the crush of everyday living, we simply don't stop long enough to pause and thank our Creator for His countless blessings. As Christians, we are blessed beyond measure. Thus, thanksgiving should become a habit, a regular part of our daily routines.

Christian believers can face the inevitable challenges of married life armed with the joy of Christ and the promise of salvation. So whatever this day holds for you, begin it and end it with God as your partner and Christ as your Savior. And throughout the day, give thanks to the One who created you and saved you. Place God squarely at the center of your marriage and your life. Then celebrate! God's love for you is infinite. Accept it joyously and be thankful.

MORE THOUGHTS FOR TODAY

God has promised that if we harvest well with the tools of thanksgiving, there will be seeds for planting in the spring.

Gloria Gaither

Thank God every morning when you get up that you have something to do that day which must be done, whether you like it or not.

Charles Kingsley

When it comes to life, the critical thing is whether you take things for granted or take them with gratitude.

G. K. Chesterton

Our prayers for you are always spilling over into thanksgivings. We can't quit thanking God our Father and Jesus our Messiah for you!

Colossians 1:3 MSG

OUR PRAYER FOR TODAY

Heavenly Father, Your gifts are greater than we can imagine. Let us live each day with thanksgiving in our hearts and praise on our lips. Thank You for the gift of Your Son and for the promise of eternal life. Today and every day, let us share the joyous news of Jesus Christ, and let our lives be testimonies to His love and His grace.

Amen

Trust the Shepherd

My cup runs over. Surely goodness and mercy shall follow me
all the days of my life; and I will dwell
in the house of the Lord forever.

Psalm 23:5-6 NKJV

Open your Bible to its center, and you'll find the Book of Psalms. In it are some of the most beautiful words ever translated into the English language, with none more beautiful than the 23rd Psalm. David describes God as being like a shepherd who cares for His flock. No wonder these verses have provided comfort and hope for generations of believers.

You are precious in the eyes of God. You are His priceless creation, made in His image, and protected by Him. God watches over every step you make and every breath you take, so you need never be afraid. But sometimes, fear has a way of slipping into the minds and hearts of even the most devout believers. You are no exception.

On occasion, you will confront circumstances that trouble you to the very core of your soul. When you are afraid, trust in God. When you are worried, turn your concerns over to Him. When you are anxious, be still and listen for the quiet assurance of God's promises. And then, place your life in His hands. He is your shepherd today and throughout eternity. Trust the Shepherd.

MORE THOUGHTS FOR TODAY

Beside each believer stands an angel as protector and shepherd, leading him to life.

St. Basil the Great

You can better understand the 23rd Psalm when you are acquainted with The Shepherd.

Anonymous

The Lord is my shepherd; I shall not want. He makes me to lie down in green pastures; He leads me beside the still waters. He restores my soul.

Psalm 23:1-3 NKJV

OUR PRAYER FOR TODAY

Lord, You are our shepherd. You care for us; You love us; You protect us. With You as our shield, we have no reason to be afraid. But sometimes, Lord, we are fearful. In times of uncertainty, we feel threatened. In times of sorrow, we weep. In times of trouble, we become angry. Help us, Lord, to lean not upon ourselves, but upon You. Keep us ever mindful of Your promises, and let us trust You always. You are our shepherd, Lord; and we are Yours forever.

Amen

Acceptance Now

Shall I not drink from the cup the Father has given me?

John 18:11 NLT

The American Theologian Reinhold Niebuhr composed a profoundly simple verse that came to be known as the Serenity Prayer: "God, grant me the serenity to accept the things I cannot change, the courage to change the things I can, and the wisdom to know the difference." Niebuhr's words are far easier to recite than they are to live by. Why? Because most of us want life to unfold in accordance with our own wishes and timetables. But sometimes God has other plans.

Author Hannah Whitall Smith observed, "How changed our lives would be if we could only fly through the days on wings of surrender and trust!" These words remind us that even when we cannot understand the workings of God, we must trust Him and accept His will.

So if you've encountered unfortunate circumstances that are beyond your power to control, accept those circumstances . . . and trust God. When you do, you can be comforted in the knowledge that your Creator is both loving and wise, and that He understands His plans perfectly, even when you do not.

MORE THOUGHTS FOR TODAY

I am truly grateful that faith enables me to move past the question of "Why?"

Zig Ziglar

The key to contentment is to consider. Consider who you are and be satisfied with that. Consider what you have and be satisfied with that. Consider what God's doing and be satisfied with that.

Luci Swindoll

The more comfortable we are with mystery in our journey, the more rest we will know along the way.

John Eldredge

He is the Lord. Let him do what he thinks is best.

1 Samuel 3:18 NCV

OUR PRAYER FOR TODAY

Dear Lord, when we are discouraged, give us hope. When we are impatient, give us peace. When we face circumstances that we cannot change, give us a spirit of acceptance. In all things great and small, let us trust in You, Dear Lord, knowing that You are the Giver of life and the Giver of all things good, today and forever.

Amen

DAY 81

Beyond Discouragement

Celebrate God all day, every day. I mean, revel in him!
Philippians 4:4 MSG

Christian couples have many reasons to celebrate. God is in His heaven; Christ has risen, and we are the sheep of His flock. Yet sometimes, even the most devout believers may become discouraged. After all, we live in a world where expectations can be high and demands can be even higher.

When we fail to meet the expectations of others (or, for that matter, the expectations that we have for ourselves), we may be tempted to abandon hope. But God has other plans. He knows exactly how He intends to use us. Our task is to remain faithful until He does.

If you or your spouse become discouraged by the direction of life, turn your thoughts and prayers to God. He is a God of possibility, not negativity. He will help you count your blessings instead of your hardships. And then, with a renewed spirit of optimism and hope, you can properly thank your Father in heaven for His blessings, for His love, and for His Son.

MORE THOUGHTS FOR TODAY

All our life is a celebration for us; we are convinced, in fact, that God is always everywhere. We sing while we work... we pray while we carry out all life's other occupations.

St. Clement of Alexandria

I know nothing, except what everyone knows—if there when God dances, I should dance.

W. H. Auden

If you can forgive the person you were, accept the person you are, and believe in the person you will become, you are headed for joy. So celebrate your life.

Barbara Johnson

David and the whole house of Israel were celebrating with all their might before the LORD, with songs and with harps, lyres, tambourines, sistrums and cymbals.

2 Samuel 6:5 NIV

OUR PRAYER FOR TODAY

Lord, You are the Giver of all Life, and You have created us to have fellowship with You. Let us live our lives in ways that are pleasing to You. We will celebrate together, Father, and we will give thanks for Your blessings today and throughout all eternity.

Amen

Confronting Evil

When you are angry, do not sin, and be sure to stop
being angry before the end of the day.
Do not give the devil a way to defeat you.

Ephesians 4:26–27 NCV

Sometimes, anger can be a good thing. In the 21st chapter of Matthew, we are told how Christ responded when He confronted the evildoings of those who had invaded His Father's house of worship: "Then Jesus went into the temple of God and drove out all those who bought and sold in the temple, and overturned the tables of the money changers and the seats of those who sold doves. And He said to them, "It is written, 'My house shall be called a house of prayer,' but you have made it a 'den of thieves.'" (12-13 NKJV). Thus Jesus demonstrated that righteous indignation is an appropriate response to evil.

When you come face to face with the devil's handiwork, don't be satisfied to remain safely on the sidelines. Instead, follow in the footsteps of your Savior. Jesus never compromised with evil, and neither should you.

MORE THOUGHTS FOR TODAY

The fire of anger, if not quenched by loving forgiveness, will spread and defile and destroy the work of God.

Warren Wiersbe

When you strike out in anger, you may miss the other person, but you will always hit yourself.

Jim Gallery

Don't become angry quickly, because getting angry is foolish.
Ecclesiastes 7:9 NCV

OUR PRAYER FOR TODAY

Lord, sometimes, we are quick to anger and slow to forgive. But we know, Lord, that You seek abundance and peace for us. Forgiveness is Your commandment— empower us to follow the example of Your Son Jesus who forgave His persecutors. As we turn away from anger, we claim the peace that You intend for our lives.

Amen

Beyond Anxiety

Be anxious for nothing, but in everything by
prayer and supplication, with thanksgiving,
let your requests be made known to God.

Philippians 4:6 NKJV

We live in a world that sometimes seems to shift beneath our feet. From time to time, all of us face adversity, discouragement, or disappointment. And, throughout life, we must all endure life-changing personal losses that leave us breathless. When we do, God stands ready to protect us. Psalm 147 promises, "He heals the brokenhearted, and binds their wounds" (v. 3, NIV). When we are troubled, we must call upon God, and, in His own time and according to His own plan, He will heal us.

Are you anxious? Take those anxieties to God. Are you troubled? Take your troubles to Him. Does your world seem to be trembling beneath your feet? Seek protection from the One who cannot be moved. The same God who created the universe will protect you if you ask Him . . . so ask Him.

MORE THOUGHTS FOR TODAY

He treats us as sons, and all He asks in return is that we shall treat Him as a Father whom we can trust without anxiety. We must take the son's place of dependence and trust, and we must let Him keep the father's place of care and responsibility.

Hannah Whitall Smith

Every tomorrow has two handles: we can take hold of the handle of anxiety or the handle of faith.

Henry Ward Beecher

When you are anxious, it means that you aren't trusting God completely; it means that you aren't trusting God to take care of your needs.

Stormie Omartian

Anxiety in the heart of man causes depression, but a good word makes it glad.

Proverbs 12:25 NKJV

OUR PRAYER FOR TODAY

Dear Lord, when we are tempted to lose faith in the future, touch our hearts with Your enduring love. And, keep us mindful, Father, that when we place our trust in You, we are secure today and forever.

Amen

Sharing His Love

Love each other like brothers and sisters.
Give each other more honor than you want for yourselves.

Romans 12:10 NCV

Christ's words leave no room for interpretation: He instructs us to love the Lord with all our hearts and to love our neighbors as we love ourselves. But sometimes, despite our best intentions, we fall short. When we become embittered with ourselves, with our neighbors, or most especially with God, we disobey the One who gave His life for us. And we bring inevitable, needless suffering into our lives.

If we are to please God, we must cleanse ourselves of the negative feelings that separate us from others and from Him. In 1 Corinthians 13, we are told that love is the foundation upon which all our relationships are to be built—our relationships with others and our relationship with our Creator. May we fill our hearts with love; may we never yield to bitterness. And may we praise the Son of God who, in His infinite wisdom, made love His greatest commandment.

MORE THOUGHTS FOR TODAY

God loves me as God loves all people, without qualification.... To be in the image of God means that all of us are made for the purpose of knowing and loving God and one another and of being loved in turn, not literally in the same way God knows and loves, but in a way appropriate to human beings.

Roberta Bondi

When we do little acts of kindness that make life more bearable for someone else, we are walking in love as the Bible commands us.

Barbara Johnson

I give you a new commandment: that you love one another. Just as I have loved you, you should also love one another. By this all people will know that you are My disciples, if you have love for one another.

John 13:34-35 Holman CSB

OUR PRAYER FOR TODAY

Lord, You have given us love that is beyond human understanding, and we are Your loving servants. Let the love that we feel for You be reflected through the tenderness that we share with each other and the love that we share with the world.

Amen

Ask Him

If you need wisdom—if you want to know what God
wants you to do—ask him, and he will gladly tell you.
He will not resent your asking.

James 1:5 NLT

How often do you ask for God's help? Occasionally? Intermittently? Whenever you experience a crisis? Hopefully not. Hopefully, you have developed the habit of asking for God's assistance early and often. And hopefully, you have learned to seek His guidance in every aspect of your life.

God has promised that when you ask for His help, He will not withhold it. So ask. Ask Him to meet the needs of your day. Ask Him for wisdom. Ask Him to lead you, to protect you, and to correct you. And trust the answers He gives.

God stands at the door and waits. When you knock on His door, He answers. Your task, of course, is to seek His guidance prayerfully, confidently, and often.

You need not cry very loudly: He is nearer to us than we think.

Brother Lawrence

MORE THOUGHTS FOR TODAY

Some people think God does not like to be troubled with our constant asking. But, the way to trouble God is not to come at all.

D. L. Moody

When will we realize that we're not troubling God with our questions and concerns? His heart is open to hear us—His touch nearer than our next thought—as if no one in the world existed but us. Our very personal God wants to hear from us personally.

Gigi Graham Tchividjian

From now on, whatever you request along the lines of who I am and what I am doing, I'll do it. That's how the Father will be seen for who he is in the Son. I mean it. Whatever you request in this way, I'll do.

John 14:13-14 MSG

OUR PRAYER FOR TODAY

Dear Lord, You are the giver of all things good.
When we are in need, we will come to You in prayer.
You know the desires of our hearts, Lord;
grant them, we ask. Yet not our will, Father,
but Your will be done.
Amen

The Balancing Act

Then the apostles gathered to Jesus and told Him all things,
both what they had done and what they had taught.
And He said to them, "Come aside by yourselves to
a deserted place and rest a while." For there were many
coming and going, and they did not even have time to eat.
Mark 6:30-31 NKJV

Face facts: life is a delicate balancing act, a tightrope walk with over-commitment on one side and under-commitment on the other. And it's up to each of us to walk carefully on that rope, not falling prey to pride (which causes us to attempt too much) or to fear (which causes us to attempt too little).

God's Word promises us the possibility of abundance (John 10:10). And we are far more likely to experience that abundance when we lead balanced lives.

Are you doing too much—or too little? If so, it's time to have a little chat with God. And if you listen carefully to His instructions, you strive to achieve a more balanced life, a life that's right for you and your loved ones. When you do, everybody wins.

MORE THOUGHTS FOR TODAY

When I feel like circumstances are spiraling downward in my life, God taught me that whether I'm right side up or upside down, I need to turn those circumstances over to Him. He is the only one who can bring balance into my life.

Carole Lewis

Does God care about all the responsibilities we have to juggle in our daily lives? Of course. But He cares more that our lives demonstrate balance, the ability to discern what is essential and give ourselves fully to it.

Penelope Stokes

But those who wait on the Lord Shall renew their strength; They shall mount up with wings like eagles, They shall run and not be weary, They shall walk and not faint.

Isaiah 40:31 NKJV

OUR PRAYER FOR TODAY

Father, let us find contentment and balance.
Let Your priorities be our priorities, and when we have
done our best, give us the wisdom to place our faith
and our trust in You.
Amen

New Beginnings

And He who sits on the throne said,
"Behold, I am making all things new."

Revelation 21:5 NASB

Each new day offers countless opportunities to serve God, to seek His will, and to obey His teachings. But each day also offers countless opportunities to stray from God's commandments and to wander far from His path.

Sometimes, we wander aimlessly in a wilderness of our own making, but God has better plans of us. And, whenever we ask Him to renew our strength and guide our steps, He does so.

Consider this day a new beginning. Consider it a fresh start, a renewed opportunity to serve your Creator with willing hands and a loving heart. Ask God to renew your sense of purpose as He guides your steps. Today is a glorious opportunity to serve God. Seize that opportunity while you can; tomorrow may indeed be too late.

God is not running an antique shop! He is making all things new!

Vance Havner

MORE THOUGHTS FOR TODAY

No matter how badly we have failed, we can always get up and begin again. Our God is the God of new beginnings.

Warren Wiersbe

When we focus on God, the scene changes. He's in control of our lives; nothing lies outside the realm of His redemptive grace. Even when we make mistakes, fail in relationships, or deliberately make bad choices, God can redeem us.

Penelope J. Stokes

Create in me a pure heart, O God, and renew a steadfast spirit within me.

Psalm 51:10 NIV

OUR PRAYER FOR TODAY

Dear God, conform us to Your commandments and
to Your plans for our lives. Create in each of us
a new heart—a heart that embraces the love that You
lavish upon us. When we need to change, Lord,
change us, and make us new again.
Amen

Called to Account

Light shines on the godly, and joy on those who do right.
May all who are godly be happy in the Lord
and praise his holy name.

Psalm 97:11-12 NLT

For most of us, it is a daunting thought: one day, perhaps soon, we'll come face to face with our Heavenly Father, and we'll be called to account for our actions here on earth. Our personal histories will certainly not be surprising to God; He already knows everything about us. But the full scope of our activities may be surprising to us: some of us will be pleasantly surprised; others will not be.

Today, do whatever you can to ensure that your thoughts and your deeds are pleasing to your Creator. Because you will, at some point in the future, be called to account for your actions. And the future may be sooner than you think.

Although God causes all things to work together for good for His children, He still holds us accountable for our behavior.

Kay Arthur

MORE THOUGHTS FOR TODAY

Christians are the citizens of heaven, and while we are on earth, we ought to behave like heaven's citizens.

Warren Wiersbe

Be such a man, and live such a life, that if every man were such as you, and every life a life like yours, this earth would be God's Paradise.

Phillips Brooks

Even a child is known by his actions, by whether his conduct is pure and right.

Proverbs 20:11 NIV

OUR PRAYER FOR TODAY

Lord, it is so much easier to speak of the righteous life
than it is to live it. Let us live righteously,
and let our actions be consistent with
our beliefs, today and always.
Amen

Actions Speak Louder

Again, this is God's command: to believe in his personally
named Son, Jesus Christ. He told us to love each other,
in line with the original command. As we keep his commands,
we live deeply and surely in him, and he lives in us.
And this is how we experience his deep and abiding presence
in us: by the Spirit he gave us.

1 John 3:23-24 MSG

In describing our beliefs, our actions are far better descriptors than our words. Yet far too many of us spend more energy talking about our beliefs than living by them—with predictable consequences.

Is your life a picture book of your creed? Are your actions congruent with your beliefs? Are you willing to practice the philosophies that you preach? If so, you are a powerful example to your family and friends.

Every day presents a fresh opportunity to make certain that your actions are guided by the conscience that God has placed in your heart. So don't treat your faith as if it were separate from your everyday life. Weave your beliefs into the very fabric of your day. When you do, God will honor your good works, and your good works will honor God.

MORE THOUGHTS FOR TODAY

Belief is faith only when it has God's revealed truth for its object; otherwise, it may be fully as injurious as unbelief itself.

A. W. Tozer

God delights to meet the faith of one who looks up to Him and says, "Lord, You know that I cannot do this—but I believe that You can!"

Amy Carmichael

Believe and do what God says. The life-changing consequences will be limitless, and the results will be confidence and peace of mind.

Franklin Graham

Whoever believes that Jesus is the Christ is born of God, and everyone who loves Him who begot also loves him who is begotten of Him.

1 John 5:1 NKJV

OUR PRAYER FOR TODAY

Heavenly Father, we trust You, and we trust Your Word.
Help us to live in such a way that our actions validate
our beliefs—and let the glory be Yours forever.
Amen

185

A Foundation of Honesty

And what about this piece of trivia: "If you shake hands on
a promise, that's nothing; but if you raise your hand
that God is your witness, that's serious"? What ridiculous
hairsplitting! What difference does it make whether you shake
hands or raise hands? A promise is a promise. What difference
does it make if you make your promise inside or outside
a house of worship? A promise is a promise. God is present,
watching and holding you to account regardless.

Matthew 23:18-20 MSG

Lasting relationships are built upon a foundation of honesty and trust. It has been said on many occasions that honesty is the best policy. For believers, it is far more important to note that honesty is God's policy. And, if we are to be servants worthy of our Savior, Jesus Christ, we must be honest and forthright in all our communications with all people, starting with our loved ones.

Sometimes, honesty is difficult; sometimes, honesty is painful; sometimes, honesty makes us feel uncomfortable. Despite these temporary feelings of discomfort, we must make honesty the hallmark of all our relationships; otherwise, we invite needless suffering into our own lives and into the lives of those we love.

Sometime soon, perhaps even today, you will be tempted to bend the truth or perhaps even to break it. Resist that temptation. Truth is God's way...and it must be your way, too.

MORE THOUGHTS FOR TODAY

Much guilt arises in the life of the believer from practicing the chameleon life of environmental adaptation.

Beth Moore

The single most important element in any human relationship is honesty—with oneself, with God, and with others.

Catherine Marshall

For there is nothing covered, that shall not be revealed; neither hid, that shall not be known. Therefore, whatsoever ye have spoken in darkness shall be heard in the light; and that which ye have spoken in the ear in closets shall be proclaimed upon the housetops.

Luke 12:2-3 KJV

OUR PRAYER FOR TODAY

Dear Lord, You command Your children to walk in truth.
Give us the courage to speak honestly, and let us walk
righteously with You so that others might see
Your eternal truth reflected in our words and our deeds.
Amen

Beyond Guilt

Your beliefs about these things should be kept secret between
you and God. People are happy if they can do what
they think is right without feeling guilty.

Romans 14:22 NCV

All of us have sinned. Sometimes our sins result from our own stubborn rebellion against God's commandments. And sometimes, we are swept up in events that are beyond our abilities to control. Under either set of circumstances, we may experience intense feelings of guilt. But God has an answer for the guilt that we feel. That answer, of course, is His forgiveness. When we confess our wrongdoings and repent from them, we are forgiven by the One who created us.

Are you troubled by feelings of guilt or regret? If so, you must repent from your misdeeds, and you must ask your Heavenly Father for His forgiveness. When you do so, He will forgive you completely and without reservation. Then, you must forgive yourself just as God has forgiven you: thoroughly and unconditionally.

Satan wants you to feel guilty. Your Heavenly Father wants you to know that your are forgiven.

Warren Wiersbe

MORE THOUGHTS FOR TODAY

Let's take Jesus at this word. When He says we're forgiven, let's unload the guilt. When He says we're valuable, let's believe Him. When He says we're eternal, let's bury our fear. When He says we're provided for, let's stop worrying.

Max Lucado

Stop blaming yourself and feeling guilty, unworthy, and unloved. Instead begin to say, "If God is for me, who can be against me? God loves me, and I love myself. Praise the Lord, I am free in Jesus' name, amen!"

Joyce Meyer

There is therefore now no condemnation to those who are in Christ Jesus, who do not walk according to the flesh, but according to the Spirit.

Romans 8:1 NKJV

OUR PRAYER FOR TODAY

Dear Lord, thank You for the guilt that we feel when we disobey You. Help us confess our wrongdoings, help us accept Your forgiveness, and help us renew our passion to serve You.

Amen

Habits Matter

Do not be deceived: "Evil company corrupts good habits."
1 Corinthians 15:33 NKJV

It's an old saying and a true one: First, you make your habits, and then your habits make you. Some habits will inevitably bring you closer to God; other habits will lead you away from the path He has chosen for you. If you sincerely desire to improve your spiritual health, you must honestly examine the habits that make up the fabric of your day. And you must abandon those habits that are displeasing to God.

If you trust God, and if you keep asking for His help, He can transform your life. If you sincerely ask Him to help you, the same God who created the universe will help you defeat the harmful habits that have heretofore defeated you. So, if at first you don't succeed, keep praying. God is listening, and He's ready to help you become a better person if you ask Him . . . so ask today.

MORE THOUGHTS FOR TODAY

The simple fact is that if we sow a lifestyle that is in direct disobedience to God's reveled Word, we ultimately reap disaster.

Charles Swindoll

Since behaviors become habits, make them work with you and not against you.

E. Stanley Jones

You will never change your life until you change something you do daily.

John Maxwell

Teach me to do Your will, for You are my God; Your Spirit is good. Lead me in the land of uprightness.

Psalm 143:10 NKJV

OUR PRAYER FOR TODAY

Dear Lord, help us break bad habits and form good ones.
And let our actions be pleasing to You,
today and every day.
Amen

Personally Acquainted

And Jesus said to them, "I am the bread of life.
He who comes to Me shall never hunger,
and he who believes in Me shall never thirst."

John 6:35 NKJV

The 19th-century writer Hannah Whitall Smith observed, "The crucial question for each of us is this: What do you think of Jesus, and do you yet have a personal acquaintance with Him?" Indeed, the answer to that question determines the quality, the course, and the direction of our lives today and for all eternity.

The old familiar hymn begins, "What a friend we have in Jesus…." No truer words were ever penned. Jesus is the sovereign friend and ultimate Savior of mankind. Christ showed enduring love for His believers by willingly sacrificing His own life so that we might have eternal life. Now, it is our turn to become His friend.

Let us love our Savior, praise Him, and share His message of salvation with our neighbors and with the world. When we do, we demonstrate that our acquaintance with the Master is not a passing fancy; it is, instead, the cornerstone and the touchstone of our lives.

MORE THOUGHTS FOR TODAY

Certainly, no revolution that has ever taken place in society can be compared to that which has been produced by the words of Jesus Christ.

Mark Hopkins

In your greatest weakness, turn to your greatest strength, Jesus, and hear Him say, "My grace is sufficient for you, for My strength is made perfect in weakness"(2 Corinthians 12:9, NKJV).

Lisa Whelchel

At the name of Jesus every knee should bow, of those in heaven, and of those on earth, and of those under the earth, and that every tongue should confess that Jesus Christ is Lord, to the glory of God the Father.

Philippians 2:10-11 NKJV

OUR PRAYER FOR TODAY

Thank You, Lord, for Your Son Jesus. You loved this world so dearly, Father, that You sent Your Son to die so that we, Your children, might have life eternal. We praise You for that priceless gift. Let the love of Jesus be reflected in our words, our thoughts, and our deeds. And, let us share His transforming message with a world in desperate need of His peace.

Amen

Quick to Judge?

Stop judging others, and you will not be judged.
Stop criticizing others, or it will all come back on you.
If you forgive others, you will be forgiven.

Luke 6:37 NLT

We have all fallen short of God's commandments, and He has forgiven us. We, too, must forgive others. And, we must refrain from judging them.

Are you one of those people who finds it easy to judge others? If so, it's time to change.

God does not need (or, for that matter, want) your help. Why? Because God is perfectly capable of judging the human heart . . . while you are not.

As Christians, we are warned that to judge others is to invite fearful consequences: to the extent we judge others, so, too, will we be judged by God. Let us refrain, then, from judging our neighbors. Instead, let us forgive them and love them in the same way that God has forgiven us.

Don't judge other people more harshly than you want God to judge you.

Marie T. Freeman

MORE THOUGHTS FOR TODAY

Being critical of others, including God, is one way we try to avoid facing and judging our own sins.

Warren Wiersbe

Perhaps the greatest blessing that religious inheritance can bestow is an open mind, one that can listen without judging.

Kathleen Norris

Why do you look at the speck in your brother's eye, but don't notice the log in your own eye? Or how can you say to your brother, "Let me take the speck out of your eye," and look, there's a log in your eye? Hypocrite! First take the log out of your eye, and then you will see clearly to take the speck out of your brother's eye.

Matthew 7:3-5 Holman CSB

OUR PRAYER FOR TODAY

Dear Lord, sometimes we are quick to judge others.
But, You have commanded us not to judge. Keep us
mindful, Father, that when we judge others, we are living
outside Your will for our lives. You have forgiven us, Lord.
Let us forgive others, let us love them, and let us
help them . . . without judging them.
Amen

The Gift of Life

Make it your ambition to lead a quiet life, to mind your own
business and to work with your hands, just as we told you,
so that your daily life may win the respect of outsiders
and so that you will not be dependent on anybody.

1 Thessalonians 4:11-12 NIV

Life is a glorious gift from God. Treat it that way. This day, like every other, is filled to the brim with opportunities, challenges, and choices. But, no choice that you make is more important than the choice you make concerning God. Today, you will either place Him at the center of your life—or not—and the consequences of that choice have implications that are both temporal and eternal.

Sometimes, we don't intentionally neglect God; we simply allow ourselves to become overwhelmed with the demands of everyday life. And then, without our even realizing it, we gradually drift away from the One we need most. Thankfully, God never drifts away from us. He remains always present, always steadfast, always loving.

As you begin this day, place God and His Son where they belong: in your head, in your prayers, on your lips, and in your heart. And then, with God as your guide and companion, let the journey begin . . .

MORE THOUGHTS FOR TODAY

Life is too short to spend it being angry, bored, or dull.

Barbara Johnson

The moment you come to Christ, the Spirit of God brings the life of God into you, and you begin to live.

Billy Graham

The measure of a life, after all, is not its duration but its donation.

Corrie ten Boom

I came so they can have real and eternal life, more and better life than they ever dreamed of.

John 10:10 MSG

OUR PRAYER FOR TODAY

Dear Lord, You have created this glorious universe,
and You have created us. Let us use our lives to Your glory,
and let us dedicate our lives to Your Son.
Amen

Open Your Heart to Him

If you love me, you will obey what I command.

John 14:15 NIV

C. S. Lewis observed, "A person's spiritual health is exactly proportional to his love for God." If we are to enjoy the spiritual health that God intends for us, we should keep Lewis' words in mind.

Corrie ten Boom noted, "A bird does not know it can fly before it uses its wings. We learn God's love in our hearts as soon as we act upon it." She understood that whenever we worship God with our hearts and our minds, we are blessed by our love for Him and His love for us.

Today, open your heart to the Father. And let your obedience be a fitting response to His never-ending love.

Man was created by God to know and love Him in a permanent, personal relationship.

Anne Graham Lotz

MORE THOUGHTS FOR TODAY

I love Him because He first loved me, and He still does love me, and He will love me forever and ever.

Bill Bright

You will trust God only as much as you love Him. And you will love Him not because you have studied Him; you will love Him because you have touched Him—in response to His touch.

Brennan Manning

We love Him because He first loved us.

1 John 4:19 NKJV

OUR PRAYER FOR TODAY

Dear Heavenly Father, Your love is infinite and eternal. We praise You, Lord, for Your love, and we will return it this day and throughout eternity.

Amen

The Media's Messages

Let no one deceive himself. If anyone among you seems
to be wise in this age, let him become a fool that he may
become wise. For the wisdom of this world
is foolishness with God. For it is written,
"He catches the wise in their own craftiness."

1 Corinthians 3:18–19 NKJV

If you and your loved ones have acquired the bad habit of watching whatever happens to pop up on your family's TV screen, it's time to rethink the way you control your clicker. Most television networks (as well as the other forms of popular media) can be dangerous to your emotional and spiritual health.

The media is working around the clock in an attempt to rearrange your family's priorities in ways that are definitely not in your best interests. The media is trying to teach your family that physical appearance is all-important, that material possessions should be acquired at any cost, and that the world operates independently of God's laws. But guess what? Those messages are lies.

In the pursuit of profits, the media glamorizes violence, exploits suffering, and sensationalizes sex, all in the name of "ratings" (translated: "money").

So here's a question for you and your family: Will you control what appears on your TV screen, or will you be controlled by it? If you're willing to take complete control over the images that appear inside the four walls of your home, you'll be doing yourselves a king-sized favor. So forget the media hype, and pay attention to God. Stand up for Him and be counted, not just in church where it's relatively easy to be a Christian, but also when you're deciding what to watch. You owe it to your Creator . . . and you owe it to yourselves.

MORE THOUGHTS FOR TODAY

As you separate yourself from worldly things and saturate yourself with Scripture, that which is good will increasingly replace that which is evil.

John MacArthur

Do not love the world or the things in the world. If you love the world, the love of the Father is not in you.

1 John 2:15 NCV

OUR PRAYER FOR TODAY

Lord, this world is filled with temptations and distractions;
we have many opportunities to stray from
Your commandments. Help us to focus, not on the things
of this world, but on the message of Your Son.
Let us keep Christ in our hearts
as we follow Him this day and forever.
Amen

Miracles

But as it is written: "Eye has not seen, nor ear heard,
nor have entered into the heart of man the things which
God has prepared for those who love Him."

1 Corinthians 2:9 NKJV

Do you believe in an all-powerful God who can do miraculous things in you and through you? You should. But perhaps, as you have faced the inevitable struggles of life here on earth, you have—without realizing it—placed limitations on God. To do so is a profound mistake. God's power has no such limitations, and He can work mighty miracles in your own life if you let Him.

Do you lack a firm faith in God's power to perform miracles for you and your loved ones? If so, you are attempting to place limitations on a God who has none. Instead of doubting your Heavenly Father, you must place yourself in His hands. Instead of doubting God's power, you must trust it. Expect Him to work miracles, and be watchful. With God, absolutely nothing is impossible, including an amazing assortment of miracles that He stands ready, willing, and perfectly able to perform for you and yours.

MORE THOUGHTS FOR TODAY

The miracles in fact are a retelling in small letters of the very same story which is written across the whole world in letters too large for some of us to see.

C. S. Lewis

When God is involved, anything can happen. Be open and stay that way. God has a beautiful way of bringing good vibrations out of broken chords.

Charles Swindoll

Now glory be to God! By his mighty power at work within us, he is able to accomplish infinitely more than we would ever dare to ask or hope.

Ephesians 3:20 NLT

OUR PRAYER FOR TODAY

Heavenly Father, Your infinite power is beyond human understanding. With You nothing is impossible. Keep us mindful of Your power, and let us share the glorious message of Your miracles. When we lose hope, give us faith; when others lose hope, let us tell them of Your glory and Your works. Today, Lord, let us expect the miraculous, let us praise You, and let us give thanks for Your miracles.

Amen

Enough Rest?

*And the apostles gathered themselves together unto Jesus,
and told him all things, both what they had done,
and what they had taught. And he said unto them,
Come ye yourselves apart into a desert place, and rest a while.*

Mark 6:30-31 Holman CSB

Even the most inspired Christians can, from time to time, find themselves running on empty. The demands of daily life can drain us of our strength and rob us of the joy that is rightfully ours in Christ. When we find ourselves tired, discouraged, or worse, there is a source from which we can draw the power needed to recharge our spiritual batteries. That source is God.

God intends that His children lead joyous lives filled with abundance and peace. But sometimes, abundance and peace seem very far away. It is then that we must turn to God for renewal, and when we do, He will restore us.

God expects us to work hard, but He also intends for us to rest. When we fail to take the rest that we need, we do a disservice to ourselves and to our families.

Is your spiritual battery running low? Is your energy on the wane? Are your emotions frayed? If so, it's time to turn your thoughts and your prayers to God. And when you're finished, it's time to rest.

MORE THOUGHTS FOR TODAY

If we stay with the Lord, enduring to the end of His great plan for us, we will enjoy the rest that results from living in the kingdom of God.

Serita Ann Jakes

Some of us would do more for the Lord if we did less.

Vance Havner

Thou hast formed us for Thyself, and our hearts are restless till they find rest in Thee.

St. Augustine

Come to me, all you who are weary and burdened, and I will give you rest. Take my yoke upon you and learn from me, for I am gentle and humble in heart, and you will find rest for your souls. For my yoke is easy and my burden is light.

Matthew 11:28-30 NIV

OUR PRAYER FOR TODAY

Dear Lord, when we're tired, give us the wisdom to do
the smart thing: give us the wisdom to rest.
Amen

Still Learning

The Lord says, "I will make you wise and show you
where to go. I will guide you and watch over you."

Psalm 32:8 NCV

Whether you're twenty-two or a hundred and two, you've still got lots to learn. Even if you're a very wise person, God isn't finished with you yet. Why? Because lifetime learning is part of God's plan—and He certainly hasn't finished teaching you some very important lessons.

Do you seek to live a life of righteousness and wisdom? If so, you must continue to study the ultimate source of wisdom: the Word of God. You must associate, day in and day out, with godly men and women. And, you must act in accordance with your beliefs. When you study God's Word and live according to His commandments, you will become wise . . . and you will be a blessing to your friends, to your family, and to the world.

Our first step toward gaining God's wisdom is to know what we do not know; that is, to be aware of our shortcomings.

Dianna Booher

MORE THOUGHTS FOR TODAY

The essence of wisdom, from a practical standpoint, is pausing long enough to look at our lives—invitations, opportunities, relationships—from God's perspective. And then acting on it.

Charles Stanley

The fruit of wisdom is Christlikeness, peace, humility, and love. And, the root of it is faith in Christ as the manifested wisdom of God.

J. I. Packer

Wisdom is the principal thing; therefore get wisdom. And in all your getting, get understanding.

Proverbs 4:7 NKJV

OUR PRAYER FOR TODAY

We seek wisdom, Lord, not as the world gives,
but as You give. Lead us in Your ways and teach us from
Your Word so that, in time, our wisdom might glorify
Your kingdom and Your Son.
Amen